MIX
PRO
AUDIO
SERIES

MUSIC PRODUCERS

CONVERSATIONS WITH TODAY'S TOP RECORD MAKERS

▼▼▼

EDITOR: TERRI STONE
SERIES EDITOR: DAVID SCHWARTZ

HL Hal Leonard Publishing Corporation

Library of Congress Catalog Card Number: 92-070769

These articles were previously published in a somewhat different form in *Mix* magazine.

Book design by Michael Zipkin.

Production staff: Brad Smith, general manager; Todd Souvignier, editorial manager; Georgia George, production director.

Special thanks to *Mix* editors: Alex Behr, Adam Beyda, Karen Margroff Dunn, Jeffry Forlenza, Blair Jackson, Tom Kenny, George Petersen, Paul Potyen, Jeanne Zanussi.

Additional thanks to Chris Albano and J.J. Jenkins at Hal Leonard Publishing Corporation.

Jeff Lynne cover photo by Jeffrey Katz; Phil Ramone and Hugh Padgham cover photos courtesy of Solid State Logic Inc.; George Martin cover photo by Hideo Oida.

-

MIXBOOKS
6400 Hollis St., Suite 12
Emeryville, CA 94608
(510) 653-3307

Also from MixBooks:
Hal Blaine and the Wrecking Crew
Studio Life
Auditory Perception Course

MixBooks is a division of Act III Publishing

ISBN 0-7935-1418-5

Contents

Foreword

U*NTIL COMPARATIVELY RECENT times, the relationship of music and sound to humanity meant that there had to be a functional reason for the production of sound. For example, sounds of the forest could only occur in the forest. Thunder and rain accompanied highly visible physical events. Sounds were part of the real world, and nothing more was possible.*

Now, with modern technology, the recorded crack and rumble of a real thunderstorm can set the mood for a love song. Or an air hammer can substitute for a snare drum in a dance song. In modern music production, the only limit to our sonic palette is our imagination.

This new ability to bring the outside world into the realm of music can be very effective. It helps us paint our individual concepts of musical images. I think it is also a contributing factor to our steering away from stark reality in popular music. In any case, recording of all styles of music has undergone a distinct metamorphosis. That transformation has led us away from presenting a recording of popular music in a "concert-like" setting, placing the listener in the best seat. Instead, we are now free to create a sonic canvas with our creativity as the sole limiting factor. In my own work, I have found that absolute reality in recording is no longer necessary, perhaps not even desirable.

In the past decade, popular recording has changed more drastically than in any other period in the history of entertainment. These changes have been accompanied by a vast diversification of the people involved in recording. To me, foremost in these innovations is a marked transition in the role of record producer.

Record producers grew out of the recording session supervisors known in the 1940s and early '50s as A & R (for Artists and Repertoire) men. These days, the clout of the record producer is at an all-time high, with many producers in the public and critical eye as often as the artists they represent. This book is intended to give a broad view of the ways in which these noted producers create their audio images.

Bruce Swedien
Moorpark, California
December 14, 1991

v

MUSIC PRODUCERS

CONVERSATIONS WITH TODAY'S
TOP RECORD MAKERS

WALTER AFANASIEFF
The San Francisco Bay Area's Hottest New Producer

"Each and every sound has its own place, its own time."

▼▼▼

BY BRAD LEIGH BENJAMIN

POSSESSED OF A friendly and humorous disposition, Walter Afanasieff is a humble guy who can't say enough about the people with whom he works and shares his passion for music. But just beneath his good-natured demeanor looms a perfectionist: a dedicated producer who takes his work most seriously.

His keyboard and arranging skills have contributed greatly to the success of several major hits recorded by Whitney Houston, Aretha Franklin, Starship, Gladys Knight and Kenny G., to name a few. With the success of Michael Bolton's "When I'm Back on My Feet Again" and "How Can We Be Lovers," both remixed by Afanasieff, he started to receive some of the credit he so richly deserves. Afanasieff then produced and co-wrote Bolton's hot album *Time, Love and Tenderness* and produced Mariah Carey's chartbuster *Emotions*.

Afanasieff is not content to take artists from studio to CD merely in a production role: "Some producers prefer to work with full bands and leave it up to the musicians to supply the music and the arrangements," he says. "I like to do *everything*. I'll create the rhythm, the drum parts, the bass lines, the keyboard parts, the string arrangements, the horn arrangements and the vocal arrangements. Even when the guitar players are in doing their parts, I'll be in their face every minute, every second, making sure they're giving me exactly what I want them to play. I like being responsible for every note on the record, which I suppose classifies me more as a producer/arranger."

He's also an accomplished songwriter, having penned such hits as Kenny G.'s "Don't Make Me Wait for Love" and Gladys Knight's "Li-

AFANASIEFF PRODUCED MARIAH
CAREY'S 1991 HIT ALBUM
"EMOTIONS"

cense To Kill." And he's paid his dues on the road (touring with jazz fusion violinist Jean-Luc Ponty) and in the studio, where his keyboard wizardry graced the recordings of Lionel Ritchie, George Benson, Patti Labelle, the Four Tops, the Pointer Sisters, Natalie Cole, Barbra Streisand, Regina Belle, Jermaine Stewart, Clarence Clemmons, Teena Marie, D'Atra Hicks and Eddie Murphy.

His contributions to movie scores include keyboard credits on the soundtracks of *91/2 Weeks*, *Beverly Hills Cop II*, *License To Kill*, *Mannequin*, *Innerspace* and *Everybody's All-American*. TV credits include keys for *Max Headroom* and ad spots for Levi's, California Raisins, Taco Bell and a host of others.

▼▼▼

MIX: Where does it all start for you? Where do your productions begin?

AFANASIEFF: Definitely on the computer. We like to use Mac IIs with Vision or Performer, depending on who's actually running the program. I'm a big fan of sequencing technology. We usually program for a couple of days first, get the arrangement down and then go to tape. Tape is the very last step, though, after the arrangement is exactly as I want it. Because sometimes I'll prepare arrangements for artists, and if they decide to change keys...well...If you're already on tape, you're cooked—no way to transpose without re-recording. I like computers and hard disks: the digital domain. No fuss, no muss, easy to transpose. No analog punch-ins or razor blades.

Although we rely heavily on sequencers, we always go for that "live" sound. There's a lot of straight-ahead keyboard playing on all of my projects. We program in real time, never in step time. Real performance lends itself to the live feeling of the track, and we don't even quantize those parts. Generally, the only parts we quantize are some of the most basic rhythm tracks, but never the fills or embellishments.

I like to start with the drums. We have a huge arsenal of synths and samplers: a Fairlight, Akai S1000, Roland S-770 and everything in between. We start from the ground up and get the best drum sounds for the particular song. I'll go through and pick out the most interesting kick drum, and then we'll get the snare or maybe two snares, the toms, hi-hats, etc. We'll just work our way up individually, locating each sound as we need it in the mix. Each and every sound has its own place, its own time. I'll sit there and put it all together as a puzzle. I don't like to be redundant with parts or sounds: I don't like the same instruments or percussion continually playing on the same beat. If the snare is playing on two, sometimes I'll add a tambourine with it on four. If the beat is driving, I'll put the kick on all four beats. If there's a cowbell part, congas and TR-808 drums, then you find a slot for every percussion instrument you've selected and make it work. I start creating sound ideas to fill the slots up as interestingly as possible; that's where you start getting a little more innovative. Instead of a handclap, maybe I'll use a tambourine tuned two or three octaves down, or maybe use a hard anvil or pipe sound, or a backward effect and put them here and there, filling the rhythmic slots.

After that, we sequence bass parts, fill in with the keys and then go back to bass and drums on the outro, letting them both add more fills.

Gradually, the strings, horns and other parts all come together. Then we go to tape or direct-to-hard disk.

MIX: I notice you mention the word "we" a lot. Do you have a regular production staff or other players with whom you work on a regular basis?

AFANASIEFF: Yes. While I am the sole producer on my projects and play all the parts, I also work with two wonderful programmers who sit right alongside me. It's sort of like flying a ship. I'm in the middle as a pilot, and I've got these two great co-pilots on either side of me telling me when there's turbulence up ahead.

Ren Klyce is both a sound designer and programmer—and a great musician. Louis Biancaniello is an incredible songwriter, programmer and keyboard player, as well as a producer in his own right. They are both highly dedicated. There's also Dana Jon Chappelle, my engineer. He's always a great asset on any project.

MIX: I see you're a big fan of the various synth and sampling technologies. Are there any instruments that you use on a consistent basis to get specific tones or sounds?

AFANASIEFF: Among the three of us, we have just about everything out there. The Peavey DPM3 is an incredible instrument. I've been involved a little bit in the development of this keyboard. It's got this enormous bottom. We're using it more and more for drums, pianistic chords with good low end, and keyboard bass. We use all kinds of samplers—everything from a Roland 330 up to an NED Synclavier—at The Plant, where I do most of my work. I usually go first to the Korg M1 for the more ethereal, voicey, bell-like pad sounds, and then the Roland D-50 for texturing and layering bells and string pads. For crisper, more percussive sounds I use the Yamaha DX7II, TX802 and the TX816 rack for little tick-tock sequence parts, for adding punch to bass parts and bite to bell parts. The Yamaha MIDI Grand is exciting. It's such an incredible instrument. Push down the pedal and you can have any blend, any sound you want coming out of the speakers. It's really conducive to film scoring. Eventually, I believe we'll see just one keyboard/controller and a computer capable of generating all these sounds, or even everything in one box like a mini-Synclavier.

MIX: You mentioned something about working at The Plant Studios in Sausalito, Calif. Do you work there often?

AFANASIEFF: Yes. I especially love working in Studio A. When I'm sitting in A, listening on the big speakers to a track that I did, I can hear every single instrument, every single sound, with perfect clarity. In many of the other rooms I've worked in, the big speakers don't really give me what I want, and I end up only using the smaller, near-field monitors. But in Studio A at The Plant, the big speakers are perfectly tuned, so I use them a lot to get the full power of what I'm doing.

The speakers are based on a Tom Hidley design. It's a custom-built, two-way system using a TAD 4001 HF driver, a TAD 1601A LF driver, and a White Series 4000 electronic crossover. The LF driver is powered by a Perreaux 800C and the HF driver is powered with a Bryston 4B.

MIX: How big an influence do specific consoles have on your work?

AFANASIEFF: Well, the board has a big influence on anybody's work. They all have their characteristic sound. The SSL is clean and brisk, while the Neves are a little warmer to me. Some producers are partial to the Neve consoles, but I personally love the SSL. I love the clean sound and the automation. The recall systems on both consoles allow you to move through several setups in an hour or in a day and work on various mixes.

MIX: Is there a particular multitrack recording format you prefer to work with?

AFANASIEFF: I try to program, edit and experiment in the digital format wherever possible, but I also like the sound of tape for a lot of projects. Also, if you want to work on a mix later, it's good to have it on tape, easier to set up quickly, especially if your sequencer and boards aren't set up in the studio or within easy reach and you need to remix something on short notice. The Otaris, Studers, they all have their own sound. Even DAT machines have their own characteristic sounds. Sometimes I'll work on the NED Synclavier and do everything direct-to-hard disk and then edit the data and assemble the tune. One day we may exclusively see hard disk multitrack recording, editing and mixdown.

Right now, I'm working with the SSL and the Otari MTR-100 multitracks. The Otaris are doing a great job for us, but I love working on the Studer 800s as well. Once the tape machines start rolling, I feel the need to move quickly. The better things are worked out beforehand on the computer's sequencer, the less likely we'll get bogged down while tracking, and that's the way I like it. However, going to tape and capturing what you

"While I am the sole producer on my projects and play all the parts, I also work with two wonderful programmers. It's like flying a ship: I'm in the middle as a pilot, and I've got these two great co-pilots telling me when there's turbulence up ahead."

have at various stages of the arrangement is also good, because while you're working on an arrangement on the computer, you may lock onto something really good. At that point, sometimes parts and patches are still being modified or reprogrammed, and unless you've got *that* particular version of the arrangement on tape, it could be lost forever.

MIX: Are there any particular effects you like to use on your projects?

AFANASIEFF: Well, we do lots of direct recording, so of course the instruments need spatial enhancement. A lot of these keyboards and modules are capable of generating their own effects, which are sometimes strong enough to stand on their own. My approach is to first make the instrument give you the sound that you want, modify it if necessary and then add any effects through your outboard gear. In all honesty, Dana handles the settings on the outboard gear better than I do. We've been working together so long that he just knows what I like. On every session, he documents all settings and configurations of the synths, including the patches, effects settings and modified parameters. He also documents the outboard and console settings, although the SSL does a lot of that for us. I love the AMS, the Lexicons and the Eventides. We use all sorts of configurations of reverbs, but I particularly love the AMS reverbs for most everything.

I'll go to the Lexicon PCM42 for my delays, plus other Lexicon reverbs and the Eventides to create additional effects and the overall coloring of the track.

MIX: How would you describe your sound?

AFANASIEFF: My productions are all very big and very strong. I like to cover the full spectrum of sound—very strong on the bottom end and very strong on the high end. I rely mostly on the strength of the arrangement, but a lot of great things come out in the mix, and Dana is the guy who opens it up for me at that stage.

MIX: How does it feel to be stepping out from behind the shadow of producer Narada Michael Walden?

AFANASIEFF: I've learned a great deal from Narada, but now it's time to leave the nest and set up my own shop. I will always draw upon what I've learned from him; however, I've been anxious to do things on my own for a while, and now's a great time for me to move on.

MIX: Any plans for the future?

AFANASIEFF: I have some ideas for developing new talent. I'd like to be the force behind the next big San Francisco Bay Area rock band—you know, hand-picked young guys who are all great musicians. I'd write with them, produce a record and hopefully they'd be a great success. They'd have the raw power of Led Zeppelin and the intelligence of Toto: just the ultimate *musical* rock band. I'm also looking forward to writing for and producing as many artists as possible.

The Bay Area has given me everything I have up until now. I definitely plan to stay here, improve on what I've done, and take it all the way.

▼▼▼

Don Dixon
Southern Indie Roots

"*A perfect recording is not always the correct recording.*"

▼▼▼

BY GODREY CHESHIRE

L EGEND HAS IT that Don Dixon got his start as a producer at the tender age of four, belting out a rendition of "Tutti Frutti" in a record-o-matic booth in his South Carolina hometown. Even discounting that precocious debut, he started young. While playing in an array of high school jazz and rock bands, he began learning the craft of recording, working with artists ranging from gospel choirs to country crooners. One of his early efforts behind the mixing board, the Toby King song "Operator," became a regional soul hit.

Still, almost 15 years separated Dixon's high school apprenticeship and his launch as a nationally recognized producer. On relocating to Chapel Hill, N.C., for college in 1969, he founded the band Arrogance, who remained a regional favorite throughout the '70s and pioneered do-it-yourself record releasing before punk made the practice commonplace. The band eventually released albums for Vanguard and Warner/Curb.

As North Carolina's indigenous music scene grew, Dixon's experience at recording made him the producer of choice for a bevy of young bands trying to get their first tunes onto tape. It also made him the obvious collaborator when his friend Mitch Easter decided he needed help mixing the first EP by a young Georgia band, R.E.M. Dixon lent an uncredited hand on that disc, then joined Easter to co-produce R.E.M.'s debut album, *Murmur*.

Although made with the same low-budget speed that Dixon and Easter had become accustomed to through years of working with garage bands, *Murmur* proved the understated sophistication of its producers' approach. The record became one of the most critically lauded albums of the early '80s and remains a beacon for America's post-punk rockers. Released in 1983, the same year Arrogance broke up, it established Dixon as a producer increasingly sought by labels as a steady, capable hand to guide new bands through their freshman and sophomore(he and Easter re-teamed on R.E.M.'s second album) studio outings. As the indie-rock movement reached major label status, Dixon's production credits mounted, eventually including albums by Guadalcanal Diary, Fetchin' Bones, Marshall Crenshaw, The Smithereens and others.

A multi-instrumentalist, singer, versatile arranger and prolific songwriter, Dixon didn't give up his own musical endeavors when his producing career took off. An album of Arrogance leftovers and solo studio jottings, *Most of the Girls Like to Dance But Only Some of the Boys Like To*, was released in 1985 by Elvis Costello's Demon label and became a cult favorite in Britain, which led to a U.S. deal with Enigma Records. Shortly thereafter, A&M Records teamed him with singer Marti Jones. He put aside his skills as "band psychologist" for a delicate, folk-inflected effort that drew upon his abilities as songwriter and arranger. That record, *Unsophisticated Time*, led to three more collaborations with Jones and to their 1988 marriage.

Between stops in a busy producing and performing schedule, Dixon and Jones reside in Canton, Ohio, her hometown. Even so, he maintains strong ties to the Southeast. He took time for this interview before a recent concert in North Carolina.

▼▼▼

MIX: How did you and Mitch Easter approach recording R.E.M.'s *Murmur*?

DIXON: We felt like it was in the band's best interest not to try to make a Thompson Twins record, or capitalize on some current trend, but to take the cool sound that they had and just present it in a cool package. The band had so many of their elements—the mystery and the arty side—that were so well-defined from the time they came out of the box. We didn't want to mess with that. We didn't want to turn them into commonplace-commercial. We felt like they had tremendous commercial possibilities, but it was going to be by their own standard, not by whatever the current new wave standard was.

MIX: Those first two R.E.M. albums ended up being tremendously influential. Do you think people may have misapplied the lessons of those records?

DIXON: It's very astute of you to note that. There were a lot of clone bands who came along afterward who were only good at playing without a lot of finesse. The thing they missed was that R.E.M.'s songs and tracks had a tremendous amount of finesse, as well as these really hook-y things. But what we ended up with was a bunch of people just strumming away and not paying much attention to each other. Granted, there's a certain amount of strumming away and not paying attention to each other evident on those R.E.M. records, but there's also this extremely hook-filled musical thing that 98 percent of the bands who were inspired by them never had. It's not something you can really put your finger on, or teach someone how to do.

MIX: Those records, perhaps, represent an aspect of what you once called "lo-fi" production. Young bands can sometimes be scared by the opposite pole. Is there a way you introduce artists to a more "hi-fi" approach when it's appropriate?

DIXON: In terms of my personal taste in recording, there are some records that *should* sound like they were recorded in a basement, because that's the appropriate thing. For other records, especially where there's more of an acoustic instrument sound, whether it's a jazz group or someone like Marti [Jones], I go for an extremely hi-fi, audiophile approach to recording. I think that young bands often are more effective and sound better with that sort of lo-fi or mid-fi approach, because it's more of what they really are. But I think that sometimes people mistake *high-tech* records for hi-fi records. There's a big difference. A sequenced-to-within-an-inch-of-its-life,

> "**I**f somebody comes up to me and says, 'Gee, what a great drum sound,' then I've failed. They should come up to me and say, 'What a great song, what a great singer.'"

DIXON RECORDING THE
SMITHEREENS' "GREEN THOUGHTS"
ALBUM AT L.A.'S CAPITOL STUDIOS

Synclavier, glossy, slick high-tech record is *not* a hi-fi record. A hi-fi record is one that's got real people playing and real space involved.

Plus, a perfect recording is not always the correct recording. Something that's got everything from 20 cycles to 20,000 cycles is not always what you want to hear, or the right thing for a song. What I'm really trying to do is make the song happen. If somebody comes up to me and says, "Gee, what a great drum sound," then I've failed. They should come up to me and say, "What a great song, what a great singer."

MIX: Do you have any special approach for working with young bands?

DIXON: I try to make it casual. If there are four guys in the band, I try to be the fifth guy and have an equal say in the ultimate outcome, even though I do have the final say if we come to an impasse. I direct people and keep the conversations going, keep people thinking. Very often, my idea will get rid of a problem even if they ultimately don't use the idea; whatever we come up with collectively will be better than what was originally there.

MIX: Do you often find yourself having to mediate between the band and the record company in situations where the label people want a "big, commercial" sound?

DIXON: Yes. Bands, maybe because of a fear of success, will not want to feel like they're having to compete for some commercial slot, or will feel like it's somehow degrading to have a hit record. Which is ridiculous. That's what this is all about. It's pop music, you're supposed to have fun, reach as many people as you can, and be honest about what you're doing. On the record company side, you've got this sort of paranoid umbrella that covers companies' investments and people's jobs within the record company. So you'll find record company people second-guessing what they've signed. They sign a band, they're excited about it, and then as soon as the band is theirs and can no longer be signed by somebody else, they immediately start second-guessing themselves about whether this band can cut it in the world-class marketplace. At which point, their safety net is the producer.

I don't want to paint A&R guys as the evil stepmothers here. Very often, the band is being just as stubborn for all the wrong reasons. What you have to do is make everybody face up to what they originally liked about the band and help them find that thing again. It's kind of like being a marriage counselor in some ways. It doesn't happen with every record, of course, but it happens sometimes.

MIX: Since you started out, how has the evolution of recording technology helped you do your job better?

DIXON: The thing that's most interesting to me is that multitracking in general is so much better understood, even by bands coming in for the first time, than it was when I first began producing. When I started out, people didn't know how it worked. The 8-track tape recorder had just been invented when I started making records. I saw the first 16-track recorders when I was doing sessions in high school. Now there's probably a 16-track in every tenth home in the country. And people understand the technology much better.

I still like the way analog tape recorders sound for some things. I do most of my mixing to digital now because I think CDs sound good, and I think they sound better from digital masters. I like a lot of the subtle things about digital technology. I don't miss the tape noise or the surface noise of records at all. That, for me, is probably the best thing about digital audio: lowered tape noise.

MIX: What do you still like about analog?

DIXON: There's a certain kind of compression that you get from analog recording. It takes away a lot of the transient peaks. For some kinds of pop recordings, softening up those transients gives you a better sound—it's a sound we're used to, anyway. We got used to it because that's the way recording came to us. It's a sound I like, so I still like multitrack analog.

MIX: Reflection Sound Studios in Charlotte has been your home base for years. What do you like about the studio?

DIXON: I sort of grew up in that studio, and I've recorded there more than any other single place. I've brought a lot of good ideas back from other studios to there, and they've been responsive to keeping up with certain things that I've found or that I want, like new miking techniques or pieces of equipment. Plus, I have a great friend and engineer there named Mark Williams, who is terrific and really smart. He can be as high-tech and audiophile as I need to be, but he will allow me to get grungy too, which some engineers have problems with. If they know they can do these incredibly clear things, they have trouble when somebody wants to do it "wrong." But Mark knows me and trusts me enough to allow me to do that. Wayne Jernigan, who owns the studio, has been extremely supportive and has allowed me to learn a lot. I've recorded all over the world, I guess, except for Japan or Australia, but Reflection is still my favorite place.

MIX: You've done four albums with Marti Jones. What have those projects taught you in terms of taking different approaches in the studio?

DIXON: For me, the Marti records are different because I've been heavily involved in the songwriting. When I record a band, I stay out of the songwriting. I usually work with bands whose songs I already like. The Marti projects have been more like my own records, where I've played a lot of instruments and sung a lot and written or co-written a lot of the songs. So I've had to maintain a certain level of objectivity about the production while still being a performer. It's taught me how to maintain objectivity when I make my own records, when I'm also the one out there singing.

Also, I've learned a lot about putting groups together for the studio, as opposed to making do with what a band is capable of. When you're making a record with a band, a lot of what you're doing is making sure you're focusing on the strengths and disguising the weaknesses, and trying to make the strengths shine. On Marti's records, it's been more a case of having an open palette. If you can hire anybody, put anybody you want in the studio, then you can create anything you like, as long as she thinks it's right. You've got wide-open possibilities. It's a little more time-consuming and, in some ways, more nerve-racking. But it involves less psychology, and it's a lot more fun musically.

▼▼▼

> *"There are some records that should sound like they were recorded in a basement, because that's the appropriate thing. Young bands often are more effective and sound better with that sort of lo-fi or mid-fi approach, because it's more of what they really are."*

GEORGE DUKE
The Ears Have It

"Without MIDI, we'd be in the Dark Ages."

▼▼▼

BY ROBIN TOLLESON

GEORGE DUKE'S MUSICALITY is well-known in the music business. Jeffrey Osborne once joked to his producer, "You know what's wrong with you? You're too musical."

Duke is frequently called by Anita Baker for arranging ideas. Natalie Cole called him for assistance on a Billie Holiday song. He introduced Philip Bailey of Earth, Wind & Fire to the world as a solo artist, and he's worked on several Deniece Williams projects. He's done Smokey Robinson and Miles Davis, as well as taking his old friend Al Jarreau into the Top 5 in the jazz and R&B charts with *Heart's Horizon*.

This well-rounded musical knowledge results from training—some on-the-job—in a variety of styles. He graduated from the San Francisco Conservatory of Music, studying classical piano and trombone, but grew bored when instructors chastised him for wanting to change notes in the classics that he learned. He received his master's in music composition from San Francisco State University and taught classes in contemporary improvisation and jazz in American culture. He led the house band at S.F.'s Half Note Club from 1965 to '70, frequently backing a then-unsigned Jarreau.

After moving to Los Angeles, Duke got his first taste of playing electric piano with Jean-Luc Ponty and was soon asked to join Frank Zappa's Mothers of Invention, where his trombone skills were put to use as well as his growing keyboard prowess. Zappa forced him to use a synthesizer for the first time, for which Duke is probably quite grateful. Between separate two-year stints with Zappa, Duke played with Cannonball Adderley's band from '72 to '73.

Duke began recording as a solo artist in 1974, with time along the way in the Cobham-Duke band and Clarke-Duke project. On many recording sessions, his name as a sideman has been Dawilli Gonga. Almost overshadowed by producing credits, his solo career nevertheless continued with the playful and far-reaching *Night After Night*.

His producing career started in 1977 with trombonist Raul de Souza's *Sweet Lucy* and Flora Purim's *Carry On*. His first big hits were with Taste of Honey ("Sukiyaki") and Jeffrey Osborne ("On the Wings of Love"). Al Jarreau comments on Duke's crossover magic: "George helped me get a breadth of material like I've never had," the singer says. "He's played this wide variety of music as an accompanist, and then accompanying himself as a soloist. There aren't any finer, you know."

And there couldn't be a better description of George Duke.

▼▼▼

MIX: Do you think the groundwork was being laid for your producing career with your early solo records, the spectrum of music and the craziness like the "Dukey Stick" that you got into?

DUKE: Without a doubt. Even my undergraduate years in school—all that theory, composition and ear training. All that stuff has really helped me be more flexible in what I'm doing now. I know a lot of guys don't read music, but reading has meant a lot to me, in terms of my pocketbook. As a producer, I don't have to go out and hire other people to write stuff out. Sometimes I don't have time and I'll get somebody to do it, but in a pinch I can sit down and write a lead sheet out, as opposed to trying to explain to someone at a session that I want this and that without knowing quite how to say it. I say, "Listen, this needs to be an A, this should be a B flat." You can actually talk music language with people that understand. And all the technical stuff really makes a difference. I learned a lot of that from watching Frank Zappa, who seemed to know so much about what was going on in the studio.

MIX: Were there other producers who influenced you?

DUKE: I never really got into producers until later, because I always considered myself an artist. I started getting into production as a means of making an alternate buck during the disco era, when it looked like the music I was playing was going to be blown away. Other than Frank, I would assume that Quincy Jones was an influence in the late '70s, but I basically just drew from whatever I heard on the radio, from whatever I liked and all the experiences I had in the past from the artist standpoint. I never really had a producer. I was always in there kicking around on my own. So when I started producing other artists, I wasn't coming in like, "Okay, now sing this note here, this is a song we're going to do." It was more like, "Okay, what do you want to do with this record? Where do you want to go?" And of course each artist has a different need, so it was all pliable and adjustable.

MIX: If somebody asked you today, could you pick out a Narada Michael Walden- or Keith Olsen-produced song?

DUKE: Most producers have a pretty identifiable sound. The main difference between me and most of the contemporary producers is that I do so many different types of music that it would be a little more difficult to tell

my productions from one another. Going from Miles Davis to Smokey Robinson, for example. If you heard the song I did for Miles and the one I did for Smokey you'd swear they were produced by different people. That's diversity. That's what I've always tried to achieve in my playing and my music, and I've tried to adapt that to production as well.

MIX: How do you explain being a great player and being able to cross over to successful producing? Not everyone can do that.

DUKE: A lot of it has to do with being able to get along with people and being able to listen and perceive what's going on in somebody's head. Sometimes you get singers in and they've got a thousand things going through their minds, and they're not putting out their best. You've got to find some way to get a spark out of them and get them into the song so that it's like they're making the decisions. Even though you may be making suggestions and guiding the ship along in a certain way, you have to convince them that they have made the right decision. And once they make a decision, something clicks on in their head, something changes. As soon as that confidence comes back, it's like another singer stepped into the room.

MIX: You and Jeffrey Osborne seem to work well together.

DUKE: He was very involved with what was going on in the studio. I learned as much from him as he learned from me. When you're dealing with a singer like that, there's almost nothing to say. He goes in and sings, and two takes later you've got it. He had a lot of confidence, and an innate sense about which way to go with his own career. At that time he was very unique, and I was glad to have that opportunity to work with him.

     I have to admit that the third record I did with him, *Don't Stop*, suffered from not having as much involvement from Jeffrey as *Stay With Me Tonight* did. I have to accept blame for that, even though it was a successful record. He had gotten so hot and was flying up to perform at Vegas and Tahoe and wasn't around for enough of the record.

MIX: What do you spend the most time on in the studio?

DUKE: I'll spend a lot of time on a mix, but in the final analysis, I'd probably spend more time on a vocal. If the vocalist is the lead and we don't sell it with the vocal, we ain't got a shot whether the mix is right or not. A mix can be bad and the vocal can be happening and you've still got a record. So the basic record has to be there, which generally doesn't take that much time for me. And as long as I can get the artist in that work mode and believing that we're going for something special, then we're generally okay.

MIX: How much of a good sound in the studio is equipment, and how much of it is the ears in the booth?

DUKE: Whether you're talking about samples or live musicians, you've got to start with something that's good. If you've got a great sample, then you don't need to use as much EQ or anything else. So if you start off with a good source, it's automatically going to sound better. Plus I have a great engineer, Erik Zobler.

MIX: If you had to choose, would you prefer good equipment and a bad engineer or bad equipment and a good engineer?

DUKE: I'd rather have bad equipment and a good engineer, because you can't replace somebody who's got an ear. In my studio, I've got what I call a "Poor Man's Massenburg" setup. I have a Series 3B console, which is an old Soundcraft, before they changed over to the SSL people. The Series 3B we use for playback almost exclusively. There may be an occasion where we record through the board, but very seldom. Normally we go through George Massenburg preamps, or another kind—one that was actually built by my engineer—depending on what we're recording and what we're looking for out of the preamp; something very transparent, not quite as sophisticated or as wide, or whatever. We go through various limiters or other paraphernalia, depending on what we need for the sound we're dealing with, and go right into the Mitsubishi. I have a 32-track digital tape machine. And on occasion I'll just record right out of the Synclavier into the Mitsubishi.

MIX: What first piece of equipment would you buy if you were starting up a studio?

DUKE: A Synclavier, because that's a studio all in one. The Korg M1 is great, too. But when I recorded Jeffrey Osborne's first record, all those great songs except for a couple were done in my office, where I had my secretary working, my coffee machine and my refrigerator. I had switches put on so I could turn the refrigerator and clocks off. I used to put foam in the windows. I'd move my secretary's desk, and we would put Jeffrey over there and put a mic up in front of him and let him sing. Close the door. And I had to make sure my kids didn't walk on the floor up above. There was no Synclavier at that time. In terms of recording you don't always need something real elaborate to make something happen. But to bring it back to the Synclavier, you've got a very strong medium for recording, a strong workstation for doing everything you need. Even without direct-to-disk, you can definitely do a complete track on the Synclavier. That's what I've been doing for years.

MIX: I can understand a producer having a core of musicians and wanting to use them on a lot of different records. Do you feel any obligation to use new guys, keep bringing in fresh players?

DUKE: No, I don't feel an obligation to do that. In terms of my work, my responsibility is to the record company and to the artists. And that's pretty much where the buck stops. I have to give the artist, in the most efficient way possible, the product they're looking for, and that may mean using the guys that I use all the time. I'm reluctant to use musicians I don't know, because I can call so and so and they'll come over here and be in and out in ten minutes. I will experiment more on my own records, because it's my budget and that's different. But when I'm dealing as a producer with other people's records, I've got their money in my pocket, and I don't want to experiment with it.

MIX: Has MIDI changed things at your studio?

DUKE: Oh, tremendously. Without MIDI, we'd be in the Dark Ages. I remember going onstage and playing without MIDI, and I don't know how I ever did it. If we'd had MIDI when I was with Frank Zappa, can you imagine what could have happened in that band? I wonder some-

"I'll spend a lot of time on a mix, but in the final analysis, I'd probably spend more time on a vocal. A mix can be bad and the vocal can be happening and you've still got a record."

times. I think it's just the greatest innovation of this century. It's absolutely essential. I've got everything going through a big Cooper MIDI switcher, and everything is hooked up to the Synclavier through that, so I can switch it around any way I want to. I've got my Minimoog and all my stuff MIDIed up to this unit, and I can pretty much choose what I want to do and run it down any track that I decide to use on the Synclavier. I love the idea of rack-mounting everything and having it come through one or two keyboards.

MIX: In what ways does your own music benefit by you being a producer?

DUKE: I did a couple of songs for Barry Manilow. A lot of people would say, "Wow, that's weird." But I tell you, from working with Barry you learn something. From working with Frank I learned something. From working with Miles. Whoever. From working with Smokey Robinson, I can see how he looks at his own music and what he's looking for. And I'll take a little piece of that and put it in my music. Other than that, it's hard for me to produce myself. I'm really an artist at that point. I don't get on myself as hard as I probably should, except about my vocals. My voice in general has gotten a lot better because of that, but in terms of overall concept of albums, that's kind of tough, because I'm really an artist first, and the producer takes a back seat. I tell him to sit down, because this is my record and my time to get crazy and do what I want to do.

▼▼▼

DAVE EDMUNDS
Back to Basics

I T'S BEEN SOME 24 years since Welsh rocker Dave Edmunds first roared up the charts as a member of the band Love Sculpture with his turbo-charged version of Khatchaturian's "Sabre Dance." Since then, the 48-year-old singer/guitarist/producer has had a long and distinguished career, spanning solo hits such as "I Hear You Knocking" and "Queen of Hearts," as well a tenure with Rockpile, the forceful and hard-rocking quartet formed with Nick Lowe, Terry Williams and Billy Bremner.

During the '80s, Edmunds also emerged as one of the most in-demand producers in the music business. His production credits include albums for such diverse artists as the Everly Brothers, Dion, Stray Cats, k.d. lang, Status Quo, Shakin' Stevens and Mason Ruffner. He also produced an album for his old mate Nick Lowe, and in 1989, after a five-year absence as an artist, he released a new album of his own, *Closer to the Flame*. Self-produced and nearly two years in the making, the album is a fiery celebration of his rock 'n' roll roots.

Sitting in the Capitol Tower in Hollywood, Edmunds is dressed all in black, but in a happy mood nonetheless. He talked to *Mix* about his career, his music and his production work.

▼▼▼

MIX: What kind of music did you listen to growing up?
EDMUNDS: Rock 'n' roll was my big influence, especially all the main artists such as Chuck Berry, Elvis, Jerry Lee Lewis, Gene Vincent, Fats Domino, Little Richard, Carl Perkins, Buddy Holly, the Everly Brothers. I loved their music and that sound, that feel, the moment I heard it, and it's stayed with me.
MIX: How did you get started in the business?
EDMUNDS: I always liked having a band, and eventually my group, The Raiders, became the most popular group in South Wales. It was a trio, and we did quite well. Then I got to know Kingsley Ward, who'd built Rockfield Studio on his farm with his brother, and we made a record there, and then it got released on EMI. So I got into the business almost through the back door. I didn't move up to London and get a proper manager like everyone else; I just submitted this tape and got a deal that way.
MIX: You were closely associated with Rockfield in the early days. Tell us a bit about the studio and recording there.
EDMUNDS: A lot of people think that I owned it. I'm not sure how that story started, except that I always talked about the studio rather than some of the early records. The studio was and still is owned by Kingsley, and we

"**I** *try to capture the moment rather than laboring away at overdubbing and layering sounds.*"

▼▼▼

BY IAIN BLAIR

had this idea of making records like Motown or Stax, who were my big influences. It was great fun recording there in the old days, because it was basically just two mono machines in a barn on this farm. Kingsley and Charles, his brother, were farmers, in fact, but had a band and wanted to make records. So they converted a barn and put in an old Philips machine and an EMI TR90, and we just bounced back from one to the other. We also had a Binson Echo and a Grampian spring reverb, and one Neumann mic and a few Shure live mics. That was it—nothing very sophisticated, but we got a great sound. And soon after the first hit, they put in a Levers Rich 8-track, a huge, monstrous machine that we had to kick every time we spooled back to make it work. And then we'd use the EMI TR90 for ADT, echo and other effects.

MIX: At Rockfield, you came up with an instantly identifiable sound on your cover hits of "I Hear You Knocking," "Baby, I Love You" and "Born To Be With You." Can you comment on that sound?

EDMUNDS: "I Hear You Knocking" by Smiley Lewis was just one of those songs I always loved and wanted to record, and funnily enough, I used the same vocal effect on "Don't Talk To Me" on my new album, with a lot of compression and a lot of mid-frequency—2.8 and 5.6 are my favorite frequencies. As for "Baby, I Love You," I had the same fun building up the tracks the way people do now in home studios, like with the Fostex systems. I did everything, from playing to engineering and mixing, so I learned a lot about studio techniques and production. Also, there was no pressure, so it was less of a career move than pure enthusiasm. "Born To Be With You" was recorded the same year, in 1973, and again I wanted to do my version of the song but keep it true to the spirit of the original. They sound a bit rough now, but that spirit's still there.

MIX: When you formed Rockpile, what sort of sound did you aim for?

EDMUNDS: To be honest, we never aimed for anything except going out for a drink afterwards! Musically, I guess we aimed for that urgent, raw, rock 'n' roll sound that makes you get up and dance, but it was never that calculated. We played and sounded like that because that's how we felt. It was almost more a case of a bunch of friends who got together, and Rockpile was the result.

MIX: How did you come to record "Girl Talk" and "Queen of Hearts"?

EDMUNDS: Elvis Costello was managed by Jake Riviera, who also managed Nick Lowe, and Elvis just gave me the cassette of "Girl Talk" when he came down to the studio one day. Of course, his demo version was vastly different than mine. It was just him on guitar, spitting out the lyrics, very fast and intense. As for "Queen of Hearts," Hank De Vito wrote that. I'd met him through Carlene Carter [formerly married to Nick Lowe], and he was the pedal steel player in Emmylou Harris' band. He just sent me the song, along with "Sweet Little Lisa," which I also recorded. "Queen of Hearts" was a big hit in Britain, but they wouldn't release it here, and then Juice Newton jumped on it and used a very similar arrangement, and it was a big hit in the U.S.

MIX: Tell us about your album, *Closer to the Flame*.

EDMUNDS: I started recording in March 1988. It took awhile, but I was a bit nervous since I hadn't made an album in four years, because I'd been busy producing other people. I'm also not exactly a prolific writer, so I spent time finding the right musicians to work with. Then the project got delayed a bit, because in between I was also producing some other albums. We recorded my album at Capitol Records, Studio B. We used Studer machines, all the usual gear. In the old days, I was really into engineering everything and knowing all the equipment. Now I don't care so much, and I don't think you can engineer *and* produce, at least not well. So Dave Charles, who also played drums on the album, and whom I've worked with since Rockpile broke up, engineered.

MIX: Tell us a bit about your demo procedures.

EDMUNDS: I hate making demos! I find that when you make demos, you get a great feel that you can never recapture on the master, so now I just don't bother. I prefer to work a song out in my head and then just go in the studio and lay the track down. As long as I know I won't waste a lot of studio time doing it like that, I'm much happier trying to capture the moment the first time. You know, I really believe that thinking too much is the worst enemy of any art form. You can overanalyze a song until nothing's good enough, and you lose all perspective.

MIX: Who was the first artist you produced?

EDMUNDS: I think it was Brinsley Schwartz. It's funny, because I've never really thought of myself as a "producer." It's been more a case of going in the studio and contributing ideas and trying to bring the best out of a song and a performance. So it was rather casual when I started back then, and it was always fun.

MIX: What other artists did you produce in the '70s?

EDMUNDS: Groups like Ducks Deluxe, Shakin' Stevens and the Flamin' Groovies. That last one was funny. I read in Melody Maker that the Flamin' Groovies were coming over to Britain and that I was going to produce them. That's when I first heard about it. And they booked time at Rockfield, because they'd heard I was there all the time, and sure enough, there I was! So we made a quick deal and I did their album.

MIX: Looking back, what's your favorite album as producer?

EDMUNDS: I like the second album I did with the Fabulous Thunderbirds, which also featured the Memphis Horns. There's a track, "Streets of Gold," that I'm very proud of, which is very reminiscent of Stax music.

MIX: Tell us about the Nick Lowe album you produced.

EDMUNDS: That's another one I'm very proud of, and it also demon-

> *"I hate making demos! I find that when you make demos, you get a great feel that you can never recapture on the master, so now I just don't bother."*

17
Dave Edmunds

strates what we were saying about the demos and the need to keep that spark. Nick would just demo his basic ideas on guitar and send them to me. Then we'd go in the studio with me on guitar, Nick on bass, Jim Keltner on drums and Austin Delone on piano. Ry Cooder also played guitar, and we recorded it all at Ocean Way.

It was definitely a case of capturing the moment, and we worked very fast—we completed everything in 20 days, although we then added some more songs. Dave Charles engineered, and we know each other so well that there's a lot of shorthand-type communication.

MIX: What type of producer do you think you are?

EDMUNDS: I'd say one who tries to capture the moment rather than laboring away at overdubbing and layering sounds. I've learned that I don't like recording that way, which is ironic because that's how I started—putting everything down myself. Now I like to get as many instruments down live and playing together as possible, because of that interaction. To me, the definition of a record is to capture a performance, so once you've got that basic track, then it's fun to overdub. You've baked the cake, now you can put the icing on. Starting with the drum track and then adding bass, then guitar, etc., is just so bloody tedious to me.

MIX: Who are your favorite producers?

EDMUNDS: I'd have to say Phil Spector. The sounds he got are simply mind-boggling. He's got to be the ultimate, the way he really brought depth and dynamics to recording. Brian Wilson is another giant to me. On the other hand, it's often difficult to know exactly what a producer does bring to some artists and records. I read reviews where they say, "The producer's given them this clean, crisp sound," but who knows who did that? It's all a throw of the dice, really.

MIX: How do you feel about the recent technological advances in recording?

EDMUNDS: I think it's all great, but I'm not really a tech-head; as long as I know they all work, I'm happy to forget them. I think it can often be a case of the tail wagging the dog. Some of my favorite records weren't that well-recorded, and it really doesn't matter to me. Spontaneity is the vital thing to me, and that's why I hate computer mixing—you lose that moment.

MIX: What's your ideal recording environment?

EDMUNDS: I like big rooms with lots of iso booths, and a room right next to the control room so I can plug in my guitar without tons of long leads and DIs. The luxury of space, really.

MIX: Do you have favorite studios?

EDMUNDS: I like well-maintained studios, and I have certain equipment preferences, such as Studer machines and Neve desks. And yet you can never nail down anything when it comes to recording. For instance, I recorded Dion's album on a Neve console. Then Paul Simon wanted to sing on it, and when I took the multitrack back to London, the only studio I could get was an SSL room. Well, when I started mixing, I hated it, and I compared it to the original mix, and it sounded awful. So we had to work really hard at a mix, but the end result was that it sounded much better than the original mix that I thought was great, except that it didn't have Paul Simon on it. So, using a desk I didn't like, I ended up with a far better mix! It's a crazy business.

"I've never really thought of myself as a 'producer.' It's been more a case of going in the studio and contributing ideas and trying to bring the best out of a song and a performance."

▼▼▼

BRUCE FAIRBAIRN
Vancouver's Sonic Crusader

ASKED ABOUT HIS greatest joys in life, producer Bruce Fairbairn eschews the gold and platinum records that line his walls, the accolades that pour out from colleagues and industry mavens alike, and the memories of a 16-plus year career that shows no sign of slowing down. "It's my kids," he admits, "my family, who keep reminding me why I do this—so I can go home each night and coach soccer practice."

Fairbairn, frequently dubbed the king of heavy metal producers, has almost singlehandedly transformed the town of Vancouver, British Columbia, into a musical mecca for arena-rock groups. In the process, he's trained a new generation of engineer-turned-producer, including Bob Rock (David Lee Roth, Metallica, Motley Crüe) and Mike Fraser (Thunder).

He's also a guy who paid his dues the old-fashioned way, coming up through the business as a classically trained trumpeter. His records boast a rich amalgam of rock staples: blazing guitars, brawny drums and bold vocal arrangements, carefully interwoven with well-chosen touches—a harmonica here, Eskimo percussion there. Oh yes, and lots of horns. "I always set aside a big chunk of the recording budget to pay the trumpet player," he laughs.

Fairbairn started his musical career as a recording artist, teaming up with songwriter Jim Valance (best known as Bryan Adams' prolific writing partner and occasional producer) in a band called Prism. After recording five albums with the group, he slipped behind the board full-time, and, with the guidance of Vancouver mega-manager Bruce Allen, began producing a string of Canadian acts, including Loverboy, Strange Advance and Honeymoon Suite.

Fairbairn's place in rock history was cemented with the 1986 release of Bon Jovi's *Slippery When Wet*, one of the biggest rock records ever. This was followed up in 1987 by Aerosmith's *Permanent Vacation*, the smash that helped resuscitate the band's flagging career. All at once, Fairbairn was

> **"My** *job is to help a band create the album they want to make."*

▼▼▼

BY NICK ARMINGTON
AND LARS LOFAS

19
*Bruce
Fairbairn*

flavor-of-the-month in international pop circles, with bands left and right journeying to Little Mountain Studios, a comfortable (though certainly not ultra-luxurious) complex in downtown Vancouver where Fairbairn works almost exclusively.

Fairbairn also produced follow-up records for Bon Jovi and Aerosmith (*New Jersey* and *Pump*, respectively), and teamed up for the first time with Krokus, the Dan Reed Network, Poison and AC/DC (on 1990's *The Razor's Edge*). When we spoke with him, he had wrapped a live AC/DC album, due out at the end of 1991, and was returning from pre-production sessions for the next Aerosmith project, which will bow sometime in 1992.

▼▼▼

MIX: Do you ever ponder what bands, managers and A&R people say about you when they're recommending a producer?

FAIRBAIRN: I think I'd be happiest if bands just said, "We work with Fairbairn because he lets us make our record the way we want to make it." That's the best advertisement for my work. Basically, I like to be perceived as someone who facilitates the creative process. After all, you're making the record for the band. If I end up doing the songs, the arrangements and this and that, then the band ends up thinking, 'God, what can we do?' In a way, everything they get from me is something that they've taken from themselves.

MIX: If that's the case, what do you concentrate on?

FAIRBAIRN: Production should always come secondary to capturing a moment. None of the songs on *Pump* would have flown if the guys in Aerosmith hadn't played them great initially. Once you have something good on tape, then you have a really solid basis to play around with, adding the production aspects, mixing in texture and color to the tracks. All those songs can be stripped down—you can get rid of the horns, the piano, the accordion—and still have a good album with great songs. The production is just there to enhance what the band has done. It's like baking a great cake with a lot of icing. I like a lot of icing! [Laughs]

In some cases, though, you just want the band to cook. AC/DC rocks using the bare essentials. Their sounds are separated, basic, strong, healthy, big, fat, aggressive sounds, so there's no need to mince around with production stuff. The production on their last record went into getting the sounds and actually keeping things *off* each track. These days, everybody's tendency is to double this or put harmonies on that. Working with AC/DC, I spent a lot of time questioning whether we needed to do certain things. I tried to stay true to the form, because that's what makes their magic, that straightforward, in-your-face style.

MIX: So you sneak into a project as a creative nudge?

FAIRBAIRN: Completely. I'm a lot more pro-active when it comes to getting involved with a band's creative side. I'm more of a pot stirrer than someone who sits on the sidelines and waits to see what will happen. I like to get involved with a project right at the beginning, when the guys are still putting down their rough acoustic demos. At that point, I can identify those really strong ideas and encourage them, help them along, rather than wait until the last minute when it can be much more difficult to change things.

MIX: Does that ever pose a conflict of interest, to the extent that you become co-writer?

"Conflicts are good. When you get creative people together with different ideas and attitudes, some sort of friction is bound to result. But friction can be guided to positive outcomes."

FAIRBAIRN: Songwriting is not my job. Like I said, my job is to help a band create the album they want to make. If I do happen to contribute something writing-wise, unless it's a big, big deal, I'll let it go. If I have an idea and it's going to make for a better song, then it's worth incorporating it. I'm not rewriting choruses for these guys, and I don't take songwriting credit. I'm more involved in structuring and arranging the song.

You've got to work that way, though. If you bring up an idea and the guys in the band aren't threatened that they're going to lose ten percent of a song over it, they'll be much more inclined to listen to what you have to say. If you start arguing over every chord change or bridge or word, then that's just counter-productive to the project.

MIX: You did a behind-the-scenes videotape with Aerosmith while they were working on *Pump,* and there are plenty of creative differences to be seen throughout.

FAIRBAIRN: Yeah, it was a bold move for the band to put out *The Making of Pump.* I've found many people who have been interested in it. The band pretty much bares all, and it gives a glimpse into the studio process, for better or worse. If you've seen the video, you'll notice that there were a lot of stumbles along the way. But that's the reality of making a record.

MIX: And, of course, some of the best records ever made came out of heated sessions.

FAIRBAIRN: Sure. Conflicts are good. A lot of times, if you don't have any sparks flying at rehearsal or in the studio, chances are you'll end up with a pretty dull kind of record. When you get creative people together with different ideas and attitudes, some sort of friction is bound to result. But friction can be guided to positive outcomes.

MIX: So do you ever find yourself running interception?

FAIRBAIRN: It's more like being a referee, actually. I'd rather bring a problem out into the open, so we can all do something about it together. If I don't have to say anything, then that's great; the best ref is one that you don't even know is there. However, if a discussion starts going the wrong way and could be damaging to the album or to a guy's relationship with the rest of the band, then that's where I have to step in and play the psychologist or counselor and work toward a positive ending.

You really have to be able to separate out the wheat from the chaff in terms of their comments, and you have to rely on your own instincts to know when things are falling off track. For example, if someone wants to put a 64-bar kazoo solo in the middle of the song and you sense that it may not be the right thing to do, you must question the validity of that move.

MIX: Does that extend to picking the songs that go onto an album?

FAIRBAIRN: All the time. I mean, you get a pretty good feel for which songs make the "A" list after you've spent a bunch of time in rehearsals playing them. There are usually six or seven songs that the band loves, enjoys playing and is comfortable with. These are the easy ones to agree on. It's the other five or six needed to round out the album that are the tricky ones. Those will be the songs that may be more outside in terms of their musicality, or more esoteric style-wise. They're the ones where the discussions always go down.

MIX: What do you look for in a song?

FAIRBAIRN: The thing that got Aerosmith's "Love in an Elevator" going for me was the lyric. The whole concept was different in terms of a pop song, and the strength of the riff also gave it some credibility as an Aerosmith song.

There are a few guys, and [Aerosmith lead singer] Steven Tyler happens to be one of them, who have the ability to talk about something in a way nobody else would talk about it. It lends a really unique perspective to a song.

That's why I respect Steven's lyrics so much. He sweats blood to get them. I'm willing to give him the space and time to do it, because I know he'll come up with something that's really neat and interesting. It's a little nerve-racking to all concerned when he hasn't finished the lyric until he gets into the studio, but those ideas don't happen on demand—they just happen when they happen.

MIX: You've taken a very strong anti-drug stand with the groups you work with, which is somewhat at odds with the excessive life so many of them have lived.

FAIRBAIRN: The proof's in the pudding when it comes to drugs and alcohol in the studio. There are bands out there who are smart enough to stay sober and make good music. Those bands are the ones that I've found have the best people in them, are the most successful and are the most genuine, sincere people to work with.

All I ask when a band does an album and I'm involved is, let's try and do it the right way. What they do after they finish the record is their business. But if they feel they can't make a good record unless they're high, I tell them to find somebody else to get high with and make the record with.

MIX: For a guy with your background, it must have been a kick to work with AC/DC.

FAIRBAIRN: They were a wonderful band to work for, because I was a big fan of their guitar sounds for a long time. I don't know how many times I've been working on another project and dragged out *Highway to Hell* or *Back in Black* just to listen to Malcolm and Angus Young's sounds, to see how my own guitar tracks were holding up. So it was a lot of fun for me to get in the studio with those guys and work with them and find out what in fact makes those guitars tick.

Some people tend to think that if a guy's only playing three chords in a song, that the musicianship is somehow not as advanced. But I learned from working with those guys that it takes a great musician with a wonderful touch and sense of the music to make those three chords sound like AC/DC do, and make music out of those three chords. There's nobody in the world that can hit a stronger, better first-position E chord than Malcolm. It's how his fingers hold the strings and how he hits it.

MIX: Was it challenging to get something new out of Angus Young, who by now must have played just about every solo ever invented?

FAIRBAIRN: Actually, Angus is such a beautiful lead player. There are two types of lead guitar players: one type plays from the heart, and the other type learns what they're going to do, practices it and then performs it note for note when they record it. Angus is in the first category, the kind of guy who plugs in his guitar and whips a solo off, then stands there and goes, "You want another one? Okay, sure." Open up another track and he gives you another one, completely different.

He'll do that for an hour if you want, and you'll have 20 solos with different ideas and everything. He never plays anything the same way twice, but they all come from the heart. He's a wonderful improviser. I love working with guitar players like that because they make the process so easy.

MIX: That's true. And then your first single from *The Razor's Edge*, "Thunderstruck," took the band in a whole new direction…

FAIRBAIRN: Yeah, the first time I heard "Thunderstruck," I was intrigued by it because it was a little different for AC/DC. It had several different rhythm feels going on all at the same time, and it appealed to me because it was a bit more complex.

We built up the "Thunder!" vocal theme at the beginning, and at some point we all looked at each other and said, "This would be a great opener in concert." We thought it would be great for the kids to sing along with.

MIX: So in this case, you planned the track around their live show.

FAIRBAIRN: Right, but usually you don't think about how something will work out in a live performance when you're working on the record. It was just one of those things, and I'm thankful that it worked out so well.

There are times that I'll say to myself, "If we do this, it will be a great thing for these guys when they play it live." The intro to Bon Jovi's "Lay Your Hands on Me" was kind of my contribution to their live show. I like to think that way—there are things that the kids can latch onto, and the band can use them live to translate the album into a performance.

MIX: Sounds like you've always got your audience firmly in mind.

FAIRBAIRN: Let's face it—the fans are who we're doing this for. I think a lot of people actually forget that. It was driven home for me when I worked with Jon Bon Jovi. He always would question whether particular things served his fans. We're making these records for kids, not for us. Otherwise, we might play a totally different type of music, like jazz or something. That's not to say we don't want to try and give the audience something different, or take them on a trip, like we did with *Pump*. But just because somebody in the band woke up in the country one morning and dropped acid doesn't mean we should make some weird acoustic record that nobody will relate to. People have done that, and boy, what a rude awakening for the kids when they buy this record that's nothing like the band they know.

MIX: Does the record company have any say?

FAIRBAIRN: We're certainly not making albums for record companies, because those guys never pay for the records anyway. [Laughs] We make them for the kids who buy the albums, spend money on T-shirts and come to our shows. For God's sake, let's make a record that they're going to enjoy!

▼▼▼

"Production is there to enhance what the band has done. It's like baking a great cake with a lot of icing. I like a lot of icing!"

Bruce Fairbairn

Roy Halee
Capturing "The Rhythm Of the Saints"

> *"My methods have changed a lot with the advent of digital."*

▼▼▼

BY BILL MILKOWSKI

SITTING BEHIND THE SSL board at The Hit Factory in New York City, engineer/producer Roy Halee casts a keen ear to the groove while listening back to a track from Paul Simon's *The Rhythm of the Saints*. Percolating percussion pours through the speakers, a tenor sax jumps out from the throbbing pulse, a booming bassline undulates beneath layers of congas and berimbaus as voices unite in triumphant harmony. It all fits like a glove, and Halee, an intense perfectionist in the studio, seems pleased. Finally, after 26 months of recording, overdubbing, editing, re-editing and fine tuning, the tracks are ready for Simon to lay down his signature vocals.

As *Graceland* was Simon's excursion into the music of South Africa, *The Rhythm of the Saints* represents his baptism in Brazilian music. Halee, who has worked with Paul since the very beginning of Simon & Garfunkel, is calling the album Simon's greatest project to date. It's got to be one of Halee's proudest accomplishments as well. Consider all that went into it: A sprawling, international cast of musicians from Brazil, Cameroon, New Orleans, South Africa, Trinidad and New York were assembled in different studios throughout the globe and brought together seamlessly through digital editing. *Saints* was certainly the most ambitious project that Halee's tackled, and, given the unorthodox nature of several of the homemade percussion instruments he dealt with, the most challenging as well.

Born on April 17, 1934, in New York City, Roy Halee studied to become a classical trumpet player, but got sidetracked into another vocation when he began working in audio at CBS Television in the late '50s. "I was at CBS until a big union layoff in the early '60s," he recalls. "I probably never would've left that job had there not been a layoff."

From CBS he went to Columbia Records and worked as a technician editing classical music tapes. "I spent about a year-and-a-half doing that before they put me in the studio. That's when I finally started mixing."

One of the first recording projects he engineered was a 3-track session for an up-and-coming folk duo from Queens, N.Y., by the unlikely name of Simon & Garfunkel. The year was 1964, the album was *Wednesday Morning 3 A.M.* "It ended up being a masterpiece," Halee says of the debut album that produced the hit single "The Sound of Silence."

Halee continued to work with Simon & Garfunkel off and on over the years and more recently established a tight, working relationship in the studio with Simon. We spoke to the engineer about *The Rhythm of the Saints*, a grand achievement in an illustrious career.

▼▼▼

MIX: This project was over two years in the making. How did it begin?

HALEE: The project actually started when Paul went down to Brazil with Phil Ramone to cut percussion tracks. Shortly after they did one or two tracks, I inherited the project. So the concept of going down to cut these percussion tracks had already been established. We went back to Brazil to cut more. This must've been about a year after *Graceland*.

MIX: And the idea was to capture some of the energy there in its natural environment?

HALEE: Correct. Specifically, the Brazilian percussion feel. We linked up with a guy down there named Mazzola, who's a big pop producer in Rio, and he got the musicians for us. The first time I went down there with them, there were about ten guys laying out these incredible percussion grooves. We went back several times after that for more recording and overdubbing. The plan was to create these grooves using percussionists only, and then build the songs from there, adding on melodies and harmonies later, with vocals coming last. These initial percussion grooves served as the foundation for the entire project.

MIX: What kind of inherent problems did that situation present to you as an engineer?

HALEE: It's hard under the best of circumstances to record percussion. To capture the sound of congas or anything being played with the hands—to get the tonality and the roundness of the instrument's sound in the room—has always been difficult. They sound like cardboard boxes. We had to do it all live with no overdubbing to get the grooves we wanted. There were always ten or twelve guys in a small room playing at once.

The studio we were in down in Rio was really a radio studio, so the microphones and the console were not what you would normally pick. I would have preferred having more Sennheiser 421s on hand, because I like them on congas.

MIX: Did you bring any special equipment with you?

HALEE: No. I like to go and grab whatever's there rather than use my own stuff. I ended up using as many 421s as I could get for close-miking. Plus, I had many room mics strategically located around the room, mostly 87s.

MIX: Was there any problem with leakage?

HALEE: The usual problems. But the leakage in this case was good, because it gave it a live, full sound.

MIX: I understand that some percussion grooves were recorded outside using street musicians?

HALEE: Yes, one track was recorded in a courtyard with 14 drummers—a group called Ola Dum. That particular track was a Phil Ramone track, so I wasn't party to that. I was involved with the overdubbing in the studio and any repairing, fixing and editing that went on later.

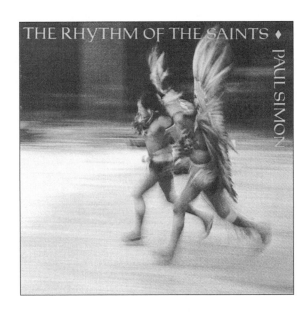

THE HALEE-PRODUCED ALBUM "THE
RHYTHM OF THE SAINTS" TOOK OVER
TWO YEARS TO COMPLETE

MIX: How did you treat those original percussion tracks once you got back to New York?

HALEE: We transferred them from analog to the Sony 3324 digital, strictly for editing purposes. That allowed us to do all types of quick editing, which is really the only reason I would use that particular machine. I'm not a big proponent of digital. But that transfer enabled us to edit and edit and edit—in some cases to go down to nine masters starting with one—repeating grooves, moving things around and so forth, to construct some sort of a form for a song.

MIX: Did you enhance the percussion tracks in any way?

HALEE: Yes. I tried to make it sound as contemporary as possible, so I wasn't against using AMS, DDL, the Lexicon 480L, the Quantec unit. There's a lot of embellishment, but I tried to do it in good taste; it's not obvious. The changes were basically to fatten up sounds and make it sound '90s. But for the recording process in general, I went for a lot of room sounds.

MIX: What was the studio like in Rio?

HALEE: It had three separate rooms. One was a dead room joined by a live room joined by a very live room, with doors leading into each room, all visible from the control room.

MIX: Which room did you record the percussionists in?

HALEE: I used the medium room to cut all the live stuff. Then I dabbled with the other rooms for my overdubs. I tried to keep everybody very close together with no gobos and nothing separating them.

MIX: What were the next steps involved in this project?

HALEE: We got hooked up with a guy from Cameroon, a West African guitarist named Vincent Nguini, who came in and played some West African melodic grooves over the Brazilian percussion grooves. And that's what the album is: West African grooves and Afro-Brazilian percussion.

MIX: You mentioned a fantastic new bass discovery who appears on this album.

HALEE: Yes, Armand Sabal-Lecco, a fabulous bass player from Cameroon. He's got to be the best bass player I've ever been involved with. I don't know if it's fair to tout him as another Jaco Pastorius on the strength of what people hear on this record, but certainly on the strength of what I heard him doing in the studio, just vamping and playing between takes.

MIX: Were there any overdubs done in Rio other than percussion?

HALEE: Many, because when we came back to New York to edit these tracks and put on the West African melodic grooves, there was room for a lot of overdubs. We would take the digital tape and make an analog slave of it, take the analog slave down to Brazil and overdub on it. Then we'd bring that back and dump it onto the digital and re-edit again. That's how the process went.

MIX: What were some of the overdubs done in Rio?

HALEE: We locked into three or four people who did a majority of the work on the record: Nana Vasconcelos, Dom Chacal, Cidhino and Mingo. They were the core of the original percussion tracks. When we went back, we got them to overdub. We also had a fabulous classical nylon-string guitar player on one song, Rafael Rabello. He's very well-known down there. And we also overdubbed Milton Nascimento in Brazil rather than in New

York. He sings a little piece in one of the songs called "Spirit Voices." We also overdubbed some accordion. And then there was the Uakti group, a fairly well-known percussion ensemble who make their own instruments. It's something you have to see to believe—some stringed instruments; some percussion instruments; marimbas; big, long tubes for bass sounds that can be tuned by increasing or decreasing the length of the tube. It was a challenge to preserve the sonic integrity of those instruments.

[The percussionists] loved to do their overdubs together. It couldn't be just one guy at a time; it had to be four guys at a time. So you had to get it when it happened. The chemistry is very important to those guys. Like on this Uakti track, "Can't Run, But," with all these bass tubes. That started out with wonderful homemade vibes made out of little squares of glass played with homemade mallets. Then they put on these bass pipes and percussive pipes. Then they put on straight percussion, like two batas. We also had a Nigerian talking drummer, and Nana played bells. It's amazing!

MIX: How diverse is the personnel on some of the tracks?

HALEE: Incredibly so. To give you an idea, there's one track called "Proof." It's like the U.N. We cut the track in Paris because the Cameroonian rhythm section live in Paris. That was two guitars, bass, keyboards and a drummer playing a foot pedal and a hi-hat for time. Then we brought in "legit" horn players from Paris. We came back to New York and put a South African bass player on it [Bakhiti Kumahlo, who appeared prominently on *Graceland*], an American drummer [Steve Gadd] and an accordionist from New Orleans [C.J. Chenier]. It was really wild. Then we took it down to Brazil. The tape that originated in Paris went to New York, where we put it on a digital machine so we could overdub Americans onto it. Then it became an analog tape and went down to Brazil, where we put on all kinds of added percussion. Then we brought it back to New York and added on female singers from Cameroon and a shakere player from New York, Ya Yo. And then after all that, Paul put his vocals on.

MIX: Did you go about this project differently than others you've worked on with Paul?

HALEE: Sure. We've never done anything like this. Never went to a place to get a percussion groove and then write a song over it.

Graceland also involved a lot of editing, but the original grooves that went on were melodic grooves with a rhythm section and a guitar player or keyboard player. The big difference here was beginning with just percussion. You'd bring it into the studio and just hear percussion, no melody. To construct it so that it was some sort of a song, from a percussion standpoint—that was a whole different approach.

MIX: What is your method of collaboration with Paul in the studio? Does he have specific ideas of what he wants?

HALEE: Oh, that's a tough one. We're just a good team. I'm strong in an intonation sense—tuning and mistakes. He's a very strong songwriter; the best in the world, as far as I'm concerned.

MIX: How has developing technology affected your methods in the studio?

HALEE: My methods have changed a lot with the advent of digital. I think we're coming full circle in that area as far as mic techniques go. When I first broke into the studio, everything was miked pretty much at a distance. There was a lot of room sound, a lot of leakage, very few microphones.

"*I'd never done something like* **Rhythm of the Saints.** *Never went to a place to get a percussion groove and then write a song over it. To construct a track so that it was some sort of a song, from a percussion standpoint—that was a whole different approach.*"

Then it evolved and records became very tight, isolated, overdubbed and close-miked. Now, with digital and its harsh, hard, brittle sound, we have to back the mics off or get a lot of distortion and an ugly sound. I also see studios becoming more live now because of this; more ambience is used. Even with symphonic records, they're going back to using just two or three mics far over the orchestra.

MIX: How did you record some of the melodic stuff—the guitar player, the bassist? Was that straight to the board or did you work with amplifiers in the room?

HALEE: Well, the bass player, Armand, has such a fantastic sound that I used shotgun cable plugged directly into the machine. I wouldn't dare put an amplifier on that bass. [With the guitarist] I think we used the Roland JC-120 mostly and also a Fender Super Reverb. And there was some direct work being done also.

MIX: How did you mike the accordion?

HALEE: That was a bitch. Sometimes one, sometimes two mics closer to it, and always one about nine feet back.

MIX: Were there any other instruments that presented problems or unusual challenges for you?

HALEE: Yeah, they have an instrument down there called a sordu. It's like a big bass drum and they put it on everything—it's generally played on one or three of each bar. The sordu is extremely low, and a good player can dampen it, double up on it, bend the thing. So, capturing the tonality of the sucker was a big challenge. I think I used an AKG 414, up close and in the bi-directional pattern. Plus, I used a room mic—always a room mic on everything.

MIX: Any particular mics you liked for the vocals?

HALEE: I used an AKG tube mic on both Paul and Milton. For all the other background vocals by the Cameroonians and Ladysmith, I used AKG C-12s.

MIX: What are some other highlights on the album?

HALEE: There's a horn section from Trinidad that plays some great stuff on two tracks, "The Cool, The Cool River" and "The Coast." Uakti playing with J.J. Cale on "Can't Run, But" is out of this world. These schooled musicians from Brazil who make their own instruments and J.J. Cale playing guitar on top of it! Then there's Adrian Belew, who plays on the Milton Nascimento track "Spirit Voices." That one's also got Nana all over the place; Paul plays acoustic on that, too, and it also has Bakhiti, the South African bass player. What a track!

MIX: What track does Ladysmith sing on?

HALEE: "The Coast." Band one, side one. They don't really sing, they do a vocal rhythm thing, kind of like chanting.

MIX: Do you have a favorite track?

HALEE: It changes from day to day. I like "She Moves On" a lot. Great groove, wonderful playing by Michael Brecker, sensational lyrics by Paul Simon. And the sound of the percussion on that particular track was captured pretty damn well. It's most representative of what I wanted to hear. The right blend of the direct microphones and the room microphones made it sound big. That was my favorite from an engineering standpoint.

▼▼▼

BEAU HILL
No Sleep Required

"**W**HAT DO I do for fun?" laughs Beau Hill. "Well, damn— most of the time I sleep. Seriously, I've been in the studio non-stop for the last two-and-a-half years, and I haven't had much time for anything else."

Now living and working out of Los Angeles, Hill embodies the mystique of the Studio Svengali—lending a magic touch to virtually every project he's produced. Previously best known for his work with L.A. denizens Ratt, Hill then hit the motherlode by crafting back-to-back multiplatinum albums for mainstream rockers Winger and Warrant.

Trained as a classical pianist in his native Dallas, Tex., Beau Hill entered the music business in the late 1970s as a recording artist, playing both guitar and keyboards (plus singing) for two different bands, Airborne and Shanghai. While awaiting the release of Shanghai's album in 1980, Hill teamed up with a friend to produce her demos for Modern Records (Stevie Nicks' label).

Those demos caught the attention of Atlantic Records head Doug Morris, who watched Hill mix them live in the studio without the aid of automation. Impressed by the neophyte producer's speed and finesse, Morris offered Hill a shot at working with his latest signing, a hard rock band named Ratt.

Drawing on his own influences (which include Queen, Styx, Foreigner, Led Zeppelin and The Who), Hill crafted elaborate vocal and guitar textures that defined the fabric of his incisive style and helped make the debut Ratt record (buoyed by the AOR hit "Round And Round") go platinum in a matter of months.

Before long, Hill was a full-time record producer, often juggling several projects at a time through various stages of production. His reputation as a recording wizard notwithstanding, Hill insists that there's little or no mystery to how he works.

"I'm not into all that secret stuff that some producers hoard," he chuckles. "We're not exactly drafting legislation to save humanity or putting someone on the moon. We're making rock 'n' roll records for people to enjoy. I'll tell anybody about anything I've done—where the EQ settings were, fader positions, which module I used, what color patch cord I plugged in.

"Seriously, there's nothing I conceal so closely that I feel my career hinges on it," he explains. "So, even though it doesn't make for very exciting reading, the secret in something like the guitar sounds on my records comes from the guitar player rather than the EQ or any producer's tricks."

Most of Hill's projects feature kick-ass guitar tracks, but the producer

"**T**he double-edged sword of success as a producer is that you get pigeonholed."

▼▼▼

BY NICK ARMINGTON
AND LARS LOFAS

29

Beau
Hill

swears there's not all that much to getting those sounds on tape. "I usually just use a combination of a couple mics to record guitars—mainly a Shure SM57 and an AKG 452EB, occasionally an AKG 414 or a Neumann U87, and sometimes an Electro-Voice RE20 as a third mic.

"In the past, when I miked cabinets, I went through all the rigmarole of sending a tone through a speaker and trying to find the 'sweet spot'," he continues. "Then one day, thinking I was pretty clever, I did an A-B comparison of that method versus just sticking some mics up. The difference was so minimal that I realized I was doing the artist an incredible disservice—using up so many hours of precious time and money—trying to find that sweet spot."

To get his lush acoustic guitar sounds, Hill *does* admit to stashing a secret weapon in his back pocket. "For acoustics, I use the same old 414s and 452s again. But at the risk of sounding like I'm giving someone a plug, I've struggled with many different guitars and many different manufacturers, and I've fallen in love with some of the new Gibson J-200 Series acoustics. So when I have to do some acoustic guitar work, I'm going to give the guy that axe and say, 'Play this!' From time to time, some guy says, 'But, hey, man—I'm endorsing Sphincter Guitars!' But if you've got his respect and trust, you can cut through the bullshit. I tell 'em, 'Look, this isn't a photo session. We're recording, and with this guitar, we can get a great sound in one microsecond. You're going to love what we have at the end of the day, so just pretend it's a Sphincter and play!

"When you're starting out as a producer," Hill says, "and don't have the track record to back up your suggestions, artists quite justifiably can ask, 'What makes your way more right than mine?' I've always lobbied my ass off trying to convince someone that a song needs this change or that. But if it doesn't work, I'll be the first to say, 'Whoops, another horrible idea from Beau!'

"I don't consider myself the imperial producer," he jokes. "If people see that not all of my ideas are sacred, that I can come up with a boner just as much as anybody else can, it lightens the attitude in the studio. That way, people are more receptive at those times when I really *do* have a strong feeling about something."

Hill's perspective as an artist often gives him an edge over other producers, especially when it comes to working with vocalists. "I was always the lead singer in my bands, so singing is obviously very important, something I relate to and enjoy. My classical background and [knowledge of] music theory have enabled me to write things out on staff paper and see how the voicings are supposed to work and know on a theoretical basis who's doing what to whom—and why.

"When we're recording backgrounds," he continues, "I take my notation and stick it right up there in the vocal booth with the other group members and sing. Many times, most of them don't know what the hell's going on, but I do that so I can keep my place in the arrangement. Then I just show them a part by singing it.

"But while we're recording, I don't hold myself to any rules—I'll keep layering tracks until it sounds right," he explains. "If two tracks are enough, great, but it can take four, six or however many we need. The main thing is to keep things a little rough so that it still sounds like people and not like someone leaning on an organ.

"I've run the gamut on experimentation, and I keep coming back to one idea: If a part is well conceived and you have good people to execute it, then you have the real foundation of a good record—there are no tricks or knobs or devices that can substitute," he affirms. "Believe me—I've tried the easy way around it!"

One of those experiments involved developing an approach to recording based around both analog and digital multitracks, with digital used more for its preservation aspects than its sonic nuances. "I've practiced the same technique for about five years," he explains. "I cut all my basics, like drums, rhythm guitars and bass, on an analog machine, because I prefer its sound. Next, I'll transfer all those basics to a digital slave reel, while doing some comp mixes—taking all the toms and putting them down on two tracks. Then, all vocals, keyboards and special effects get cut on the digital machine. That way, I only run the analog reel once when I record, and once when I make the slave reel. I never put it up again until I need the original basic tracks to mix the record."

Why bother with such matters? Hill says, "In the days before digital, I struggled with the fact that you can often lose high end on certain things like cymbals because of the physical properties of running analog tape

> *"**I**'ve learned to trust my instincts during those flash moments of a creative burst. I have no problem committing to something forever and saying, 'This is the sound, this is what we're going to go with.'"*

FRONT ROW: THE STORM BAND MEMBERS (LEFT TO RIGHT): ROSS VALORY, GREG ROLIE AND KEVIN CHALFANT. BACK ROW: PRODUCER BEAU HILL AND ENGINEER JIMMY HOYSON

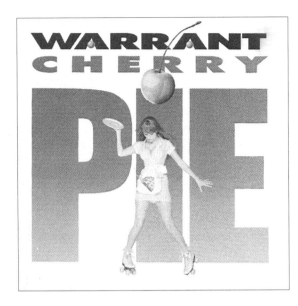

HILL PRODUCED WARRANT'S SECOND
ALBUM, "CHERRY PIE," RELEASED
IN 1990

> "*If two tracks are enough, great, but it can take four, six or however many we need. The main thing is to keep things a little rough so that it still sounds like people and not like someone leaning on an organ.*"

back and forth over the tape heads.

"For things like solos," he explains, "I'll usually add effects in the mixing stage, but on vocals, keyboards and drums, I commit to an effect very early on and print it right to tape. I have no problem committing to something forever and saying, 'This is the sound, this is what we're going to go with.' Besides, most of the people in the room usually say, 'This is great—let's capture it right this minute!' It's like taking a Polaroid."

Though more than content with his recent successes on the great rock 'n' roll playing field, we'd heard some rumors about an impending move to the front office. "It's true," Hill confirms, "I'm going into partnership with Ted Fields and Jimmy Iovine, and we're starting our own record company."

Does this have anything to do with getting out of the heavy metal gridlock he's been stuck in? "Actually, after the first couple of Ratt records, I tried to branch out and do other types of music," Hill recollects. "I've worked with Chaka Khan, Steve Walsh, Bob Dylan, Eric Clapton, Roger Daltry, Gary Moore and Fiona, doing anything I could do.

"Believe it or not, my favorite artist in the whole world is Peter Gabriel. His music is exactly where I live as a musician and a writer. But the double-edged sword of success as a producer is that you get pigeonholed. As much as I want to do a Whitney Houston record, and as much as I think I would be tremendous doing a record with her, she would never for two seconds consider me, because I'm a heavy metal hack.

"Unfortunately," he continues, "heavy metal producers and groups are kind of looked down on as the leper colony of the music industry. I understand hard rock or heavy metal, if that's what you choose to call it, because I play it, write it and really love it. There's no denying that it got a little monosyllabic for a while, but I finally realized that this is what I'm meant to be—this is what I'm good at. It's an area where I can really make a dent. That doesn't limit my scope, but I acknowledge my placement within that scope, even if it's been thrust upon me."

And as to the critics whose conspiratorial gang rushes often seem to be aimed squarely at the metallic contingent at large, Hill shrugs them off. "Mainstream rock 'n' rollers, which is what I call bands like Warrant and Winger, often get the least critical acclaim. But they follow up with the best album sales.

"Musically, it's much more difficult to break new bands right now because of the climate of the marketplace—the way that radio is and everything else," Hill says. "So I think you have to get out there with a better song, a better singer, a band that looks, moves, films and plays better than anyone else.

"I already know how to record and how to make records," he continues. "But when I take a group like Warrant or Winger and help them punch through that barrier by making them better than all the bazillions of bands out there—with the same torn t-shirts, the same haircuts and the same spurs on their boots—that's what really gets me off about continuing to do what I'm doing. I'm one of the lucky ones—what a great job!"

▼▼▼

KEVIN KILLEN
The Engineer Becomes Producer

KEVIN KILLEN, WITH his light brogue, pear-shaped ears and tangled black hair, could have stepped out of one of Parnell's mobs a century ago, or from the Saint Patrick's Day parades that follow the green line down Fifth Avenue each March. But five years ago the Dubliner came to New York with a few years at Joyce's own Trinity College and engineering credit on U2's *The Unforgettable Fire* under his belt, only to have to seek employment as an assistant engineer for the third time in his life.

Since then, however, Killen has fostered his own Irish luck and is making the transition from engineer to producer. His console credits include U2, Bryan Ferry, Roy Orbison, Howard Jones, Patti Smith, Hall & Oates and Kate Bush. As a producer, he co-produced Mr. Mister's third RCA LP, *Go On*, Peter Gabriel's "Biko" single from the film *Cry Freedom*, and Elvis Costello's *Spike*.

At Trinity College, Killen studied construction engineering while functioning as "the world's worst drummer" in one of the many punk bands proliferating in Dublin in the late '70s. Audio engineering entered the picture in 1979, and Killen signed on as an assistant engineer at Dublin's Lombard Studios. He quickly moved into engineering dates on the studio's unique Helios console, doing jingles in the morning, rock and traditional music dates in the afternoons and scores of demos into the wee hours.

Killen then moved over to Windmill Lane Studios—as an assistant engineer once again—where a neighbor's band was about to begin recording their third LP. "I suppose it was inevitable that we would wind up together at some point," recalls Killen of the U2 sessions for *War*, on which he assisted. "We did the whole record top to bottom in seven weeks. It was fast, but that's [producer] Steve Lillywhite's style. The first day we started at 11 a.m. and left the studio at 6 a.m. the next morning, and it went on like that virtually every day for the next seven weeks. That was my initiation into what it takes to make a great record."

By 1984, Killen moved up to co-engineer of the band's *The Unforgettable Fire* LP after working with engineer Shelly Yakus and producer Jimmy Iovine on live U2 dates in the U.S. and Europe. "U2 had a reputation for using young engineers," explains Killen. "The fellow they had been using moved on to other things, and the band approached me as engineer and

> "**I**'m not really a musician in my own right; what I play is the console."

▼▼▼
BY DAN DALEY

Brian [Eno] as producer."

The eclectic Eno was at first reluctant, but a long phone conversation with U2's charismatic singer, Bono, soon changed his mind. Eno brought along his own engineer, Daniel Lanois, and the two engineers began working off Randy Ezratty's mobile Effanel equipment (brought over from the States) in Slane Castle, where the band had rehearsed. They moved back to Windmill Lane for final overdubs, vocals and mixing.

A band like U2 can subsume the personalities around it, and Killen acknowledged this when he decided to move across the Atlantic to New York City in 1984. "A lot of producers were now coming to Ireland, but they were bringing their own engineers," he says. "I didn't like London, and New York seemed like a fairy tale after listening to Jimmy and Shelly talk about it. The fairy tale part changed quickly after I arrived."

Killen knocked on doors with little success before landing a shot assisting Ed Stacey at Electric Lady. Stacey recommended him for more work and things began to happen.

A recommendation from Peter Gabriel to RCA A&R-type Paul Atkinson resulted in Killen's co-production of *Go On* with Mr. Mister at the Village Recorder in Los Angeles. While he was at first hesitant, his attitude changed after a two-day session with the band, where he found their passion for their music irresistible. "That's what makes it so attractive to me, really," he says. "You need a great performance and a great song, but equally you need passion for the music."

The Mr. Mister experience, and the LP's subsequent less-than-spectacular sales, also exposed Killen to the uniquely American way of marketing records. "In the U.S., radio has such a strong hold on music that people have to succumb to the formula of making commercial records," he declares. "The radio scene in England and Ireland is the other extreme: In the U.S., there are established artists who will get airplay no matter what; in Europe, people like Paul McCartney and Elvis Costello have trouble because it's all the new acts that get a lot of airplay. In England, it's a very fashionable industry, and if you're part of the trend you get the airplay."

Costello's name conjures up agreeable memories in Killen's mind. The lyrical bad boy of British angst-rock had done a soundtrack for an English film called *The Courier*. The music was all instrumental, and Costello enjoyed the freedom of not having to be constrained by lyrics. "He wanted that same feeling on *Spike*, and T-Bone Burnett recommended me to him," Killen says. "I was sitting in my apartment one day, and the phone rings. I pick it up and a voice says, 'Can I speak to Kevin; this is Elvis Costello.' I put my hand over the receiver and barely suppressed a gasp. Costello was one of my all-time favorite artists, and T-Bone didn't give me any indication at all that he might be calling."

Killen found that Costello's well-documented asperity is counterbalanced by a pronounced sensitivity and passion for music itself. "I went to his hotel room and spent four hours listening to him talk about music," he recalls, "and after that, I left feeling musically illiterate. That's how brilliant Costello is. I really wanted to work with him."

Killen feels that Costello had never made a great-sounding record up to then; he notes that most Costello records had been somewhat thin-sounding. "I wanted to make a record with some bottom to it," he says. "What frustrated [Elvis] initially about *Spike* was that we didn't have a really strong nucleus of players, and as a result it was rather fragmented over the first couple of months. But things picked up as players came on, and we made a lot of rapid progress.

"Elvis didn't like to spend a lot of time on sounds and ideas," Killen remembers. "If it wasn't happening within ten minutes, he would stop and move on to the next thing. You literally had to be in 'record' at all times."

The sessions took place at AIR Studios in London, in the big room with the Neve 8078 console, a favorite of Killen's. Prior bookings forced them to move to the mix room with a Neve V Series, where they mixed for a week until they played the tracks elsewhere and they came out sounding quite different. They stopped abruptly and returned to L.A.'s Ocean Way, where tracking had been done on an old Neve 8038, and they proceeded to mix the tracks there manually. "Elvis, the assistant Mike Ross and I just took a group of faders each and did it."

Killen is a man whose career is on the brink of change: The producer in him is emerging from the engineer. His strong engineering and technical background, which he considers less an advantage than an essential component for successful production, has given him a valuable perspective on his chosen field.

"The term 'production' is in some respects nebulous," he says. "Making records is a team effort. Certain producers have very strong feelings about how a record should sound, and they choose their engineers very carefully, because the producers know that those engineers are going to bring certain aspects to the record. And whether you call that person an engineer, a co-producer or a producer, it's all nomenclature at that point. The industry likes to put things into nice little boxes, but most engineers do feel that they play a large part in the artistic end of a record. It's difficult to quantify their

"*I take away rather than add in a mix. The human ear can only accept a certain amount of information.*"

KILLEN PRODUCED ELVIS
COSTELLO'S ALBUM "SPIKE"

roles and their input into a record."

Killen regards himself as an instinctive producer. "I'm not really a musician in my own right; what I play is the console, and I interpret the ideas and get them to tape. And my instincts so far have been pretty good."

He has his favorites when it comes to equipment, like "old Pultecs, and old Neve 1076s, as well as tape slap. And the GML systems. I also like to chain effects together through a mult in the patch bay rather than individually bring them back through the faders every time. Sometimes you find certain combinations work well together that way, such as a Dimension D going into an EMT 140, or using tape slap as a predelay before a reverb unit. Then you take the sum of that and bring it all back on stereo faders."

Many of Killen's credits on records list him as "mixer." But he's quick to point out that his approach to mixing is more traditional than the current perception of the mixer as the one who functions similar to a post-producer. It's a matter of bringing a new perspective and point of view to a track rather than a bunch of toys to a mix: "I take away rather than add in a mix. The human ear can only accept a certain amount of information."

Ultimately, Killen acknowledges the influence of his ancestry, even as he pursues a career in America. "I think the Irish people are a very musical people," he says. "But they're also a lot of fun and have a great spirit. I try to bring fun to a record. Making records sometimes gets all too serious. Sometimes people do their best work when they're goofing off. What I think I get from my heritage is that I understand acoustic instruments and can record them well, and I have a sense of melody. That comes from being Irish. Being Irish makes you rather even-tempered. There's a lot of paranoia in America, and so far that's not rubbed off on me. And I suspect it never will."

▼▼▼

DANNY KORTCHMAR
No Longer Innocent

HIS ABILITY TO adapt to almost any type of music has made Danny Kortchmar one of the hottest and most sought-after record producers/songwriters/musicians in the business today. A sampling of Kortchmar's productions include Jon Bon Jovi's first solo album, songs for Hall & Oates, and Brent Bourgeois. He has also produced Don Henley's solo albums, including *The End of the Innocence*, which earned him a 1990 Grammy nomination for Album of the Year.

Before producing records, Kortchmar was a solo artist who recorded two albums in the 1970s. He was also one of the top guitarists of that era, playing sessions and touring with such artists as James Taylor, Graham Nash, Jackson Browne and Carole King. "Whenever I went into a session, I tried to help out and put a little bit more in than my part," Kortchmar says. "I'd make suggestions if I thought it would help the overall vibe, so it was kind of a natural progression for me to get into record production."

Kortchmar feels it's to the artist's advantage that he is a musician. "I feel I have more to offer since I have the ability to play. With tunes I'm interested in, I sit down and play along. There's no way to get to know a song better than by playing it."

Another advantage artists have in working with Kortchmar is his drum machine programming and sequencing talents. Kortchmar does most of his programming in a 12-track studio in his garage. On Henley's *The End of the Innocence*, many songs featured Kortchmar's slick programming techniques, which seemed an unlikely thing to use when you're working with one of rock's top drummers. "Don doesn't play [the drums] on his albums anymore," he explains. "I try to make my drum program as rhythm-like as possible, because when I give Don a basic track, that's what he writes to and that's what he sings to when he writes. Once he hears it that way and sets the song, melody and lyrics to it, that's what he wants to record it to."

Two tunes on Henley's album that relied heavily on Kortchmar's pro-

> "*Sequencing is great for songwriting, but I don't know how good it is for records. I've gotten to the point where I'd rather hear real drums.*"

▼▼▼

BY SUE GOLD

gramming were the rockers "If Dirt Were Dollars" and "I Will Not Go Quietly."

"On 'I Will Not Go Quietly,' I spent a long time sequencing and programming so it would have a groove," he says. "When the samples I used to make that drum kit were sequenced for that song, something happened. It ended up being terrific, so we used it. That's what I look for: things that take on a life of their own once they have been sequenced."

Kortchmar, however, plans to use live drummers in the near future. "In the beginning, we all reacted to the technology," he says. "When the LinnDrum first came out, I thought it was a miracle. I didn't leave my studio for a year. I got a lot of mileage out of it, but after a while it just becomes a human thing, a matter of dealing with people. "Sequencing is great for songwriting, but I don't know how good it is for records. I've gotten to the point where I'd rather hear real drums."

Kortchmar met Henley in the 1970s while the Eagles were still together. In 1979, he heard that Henley was preparing a solo album and met with him. "I worked with him a little bit, and we just hit it off and agreed on the direction he wanted to go in."

Kortchmar says the first album was tough because "it took Don awhile to get comfortable with the role of 'recording artist.' He was a drummer who sat behind the drums. Now he had to become a lead singer, going by his own name, with just his face on the covers. It took a lot of guts."

From the beginning, their relationship was more of a partnership, with them co-producing and co-writing the songs. "Don doesn't really write music too much, except in the sense that he edits what he hears," Kortchmar says. "He's not really a hands-on music writer. He needed someone to give him musical ideas and different directions, and that guy happened to be me. It was really exciting for me to be writing every day.

"Very few contemporary artists are capable of writing ten great songs," he continues. "Some people can do it in a year, but not that many. It's difficult, but that's actually where the time should be spent. The hardest thing to achieve on an album is the writing."

Kortchmar says their songs usually start with him giving Henley a completed basic track. From there, one or both of them will think of a melody or a hook. Once in a while, Henley will come in with an idea and explain to Kortchmar what he wants. "He suggested a song, 'New York Minute,' which he wanted to be a little Gershwin-like, but soulful and R&B at the same time. We threw a lot of ideas around, decided what kind of mood it should be, and then I went and did it.

"Don leaves a lot of it to me, but the bottom line is with him and what he feels comfortable with," he says. "Henley is an old pro, he's infallible. I respect him more than anybody."

Kortchmar used Henley's album as a chance to experiment with different production techniques. "We tried a lot of different things," he says. "We recorded parts slow and fast, tried leaving stuff out, and brought in a lot of different guys to play different parts. But this is stuff that you can do only when you don't have a heavy budget limitation. A new group has to turn things around while the clock is ticking in the studio."

Besides Kortchmar himself, there was an array of guests on Henley's last album. "We took everything tune by tune," Kortchmar says. "For each song, we tried to imagine who would be the greatest to have. We were lucky enough to get some of the people we dreamed up."

Some of the artists they dreamed up and got were Ivan Neville, Take 6 and Guns N' Roses lead singer, Axl Rose. "When we wrote 'I Will Not Go Quietly,' I heard the chorus that Don had put with it and realized that it could be a really good two-part chorus. I suggested to Don that we get Axl. We were fans of Axl, and by lucky chance it turned out that he was an Eagles fan."

Working with hard rock singers isn't foreign to Kortchmar, who also produced Jon Bon Jovi's solo album, music for and inspired by the film *Young Guns II*. "He called me and I was really surprised," Kortchmar admits. "I didn't know he even had a clue as to who I was or what I was about, but we hit it off right away. Jon had all of the songs written when he called me, and we only had six weeks to get everything finished."

Once again, Kortchmar had a striking guest list that featured Elton John, Jeff Beck and Little Richard, though he admits that he tries not to think about the legends behind the people he's working with. "If you start thinking about it, you go nuts," he says. "You forget that you have to help them through the song. Anyone who comes in wants direction, not 'I love you, you're great.'"

Kortchmar says that the most important thing in producing is the relationship between him and the artist, and so far he's been successful in picking the right artists to work with. "Fortunately, I haven't gotten any projects that [have turned out to be] a bad match, where people aren't communicating. That's everybody's worst nightmare in record producing, because you know you're stuck in there. You either pull the plug or you slide all the way through it. I've been lucky enough or wise enough to work with people I knew I'd get along with. I hope it continues."

He also stresses the importance of establishing a good rapport with his engineers. For the past year, Kortchmar has worked almost exclusively with Rob Jacobs. "I give Robbie a lot of control in the studio," he says. "He hears things the same as I do, so we don't need a lot of discussions. He's definitely an up-and-coming engineer."

While he continues to ride high on his success, Kortchmar says he has no intention of doing another solo album or returning to touring, though he has thought about touring with Henley and performing his own tunes. "Part of me would love to do that, but I really feel if I'm going to be a record producer, I should concentrate on that. It's hard to do touring halfway, and it's impossible to do record production halfway. You either are or are not a record producer."

▼▼▼

"*In the beginning, we all reacted to the technology. When the LinnDrum first came out, I thought it was a miracle. I didn't leave my studio for a year. But after a while it just becomes a human thing, a matter of dealing with people.*"

KRS-One
Self Construction

▼▼▼

BY DAN DALEY

WE DIDN'T KNOW it at the time, but as KRS-One—aka Kris Parker—and I sat in his high-rise apartment on Manhattan's East Side, a huge comet hurtled past Earth at 46,000 miles per hour, coming within a mere half-million miles of the planet. Had the comet struck, it would have done so with an impact of 20,000 megatons, enough to make New York City a crater ten miles wide and a mile deep. This is the sort of news that makes one feel small and vulnerable, at the mercy of forces beyond control and comprehension. It's a sensation one suspects is not totally alien to Parker; he was a runaway at age 13, lived homeless on the streets of New York for six years and had his close friend and mentor gunned down in a hail of bullets on a hot city night.

The impression that Parker conveys has a certain urban consistency; on the cover of his record *By All Means Necessary*, completed under the auspices of his *nom d'industrie*, Boogie Down Productions, Parker peers cautiously through venetian blinds, wearing a desensitized, determined expression on his face that is as chilling as the Uzi submachine gun he holds cocked above his head.

This is somewhat at odds with one's impression upon meeting Parker in the flesh. Sprawled on a couch in a pair of grey patterned slacks and a T-shirt, he is unthreatening despite his six-foot-plus frame, and he is garrulous and eloquent, with little of rap's patois in his speech.

Asked about that LP cover pose, modeled after a photograph of assassinated civil rights leader Malcolm X, Parker responds that it's an image understood immediately by his audience and as integral to his approach to creating and producing rap music as a sampler might be. "The concept is simple," he says. "Are we for war or for peace? War is stronger than peace. Peace can't win with a flower in its mouth. For peace to win it has to annihilate war. It's a common biblical philosophy: stop the ignorance with intelligence. Stop the stereotype of peace being Edie Brickell [of the New Bohemians] and war being Run-D.M.C. I'm talking to ghetto kids, and they can make the distinction between the image and what I'm saying."

Parker is one of a very few major-league rap producers. Signed to RCA/Jive Records with an open-ended production deal, Parker's centerpiece thus far is the record *Self Destruction*, made by a stellar group of rappers (under the banner of "Stop The Violence") who assembled to raise consciousness and promote rap as a socially aware genre, and to counter the negative perception fostered by the violent episodes that have become a trademark of rap performances. Kool Moe Dee, Doug E. Fresh, M.C. Lyte and Chuck D. and Flavor Flav (of Public Enemy) are among the heavy rap hitters on the record. Leading up to that is a production discography that includes Parker's own *Criminal Minded*, Justice's *Ghetto Music, Cool and Deadly* and *The Desolate One*, Sly Dunbar and Robbie Shakespeare's *Silent Assassin* and the debut album by Ms. Melodie.

THE SOUND'S THE THING, MAYBE

Rap as an art form has established itself un-equivocally. But as a technical medium, rap is a different entity. And my first question to Parker is: Why do most hardcore rap records seem to revel in poor sonics? Drum machines are totally unprocessed, usually,

and the sounds seem to reflect older drum technology. In many cases, technical deficiencies in the recording process are obvious. On the other side of the coin, Run-D.M.C.'s collaboration with Aerosmith a couple of years ago boasts the sheen that most pop records achieve.

"It all comes down to money," says Parker. "The sound [of rap] basically comes from a very poor place. It was from a time when kids never had a thought about actually making a record. You'd create your whole song by a DJ bringing back a piece of somebody else's song. So these inexpensive ways of making records cropped up. And record company executives saw this and said, 'Why spend more than we have to?'" Parker estimates the budgets of most rap LPs to be between $20,000 and $30,000 for independent label acts and $40,000 to $50,000 for major labels (including producer's fees), a far cry from the $120,000-and-up budgets for major label rock and pop acts.

"You wind up with a subculture," Parker says, "a world within a world. Rap doesn't try to coincide with pop and rock. It has, on a commercial level with Run-D.M.C., but that was the first time a rap group got what I call even *adequate* engineering."

Parker agrees with the notion that rap exists in a technological ghetto. "It's like a rose trying to be a leaf. The rose never gets to understand the leaf, and the two worlds of rap and pop don't understand each other."

But then, part of rap's charm lies in its very lack of technological sophistication. What an old, beat-up, six-string Gibson box was to Robert Johnson, an old Roland 808 is to rappers. If you were to spend $100,000 on a rap record, would it still sound like a rap record? Parker's emphatic reply: "Nope!"

Parker skips pre-production in most cases, heading directly into the SSL room at Power Play Studios in Queens, N.Y. This room, he says, is really the only one built with rap in mind. He likes the SSL automation and comments, "It makes you lazy, but it makes things quick, and with rap it's the feeling that you want to capture." The SSL provides what he calls an "authoritative" sound, and given the budgets he is typically constrained by, time is of the essence.

Parker says that engineers who work rap dates should "take 75 percent of what you've learned as an engineer and throw it in the garbage." As an example, he proudly cites one of his favorite recording techniques: "I like to distort the bass levels. There's actually an art to distortion; there's an art to a kick drum that's too loud. If the kick isn't 'boom, boom, boom,' you're not in the competition."

Parker's sound is self-defined as "a reggae, hip hop type of sound, hard-based with social lyrics, and not played on radio except for really commercial stuff, like 'I'm Gonna Get You, Sucka.'"

Rap sounds seem to undergo periodic evolutions, driven less by technological changes than by the intensely personal aspect of what a sound represents to an artist. Not that trends don't manifest themselves as clichés — James Brown's "oww" is perhaps the most sampled piece of sound in creation. But, as Parker puts it, "Everyone is always hunting for the new boom. In the rap industry, not having an SP-12 [E-mu sampling drum machine] is like going to school with no books. Get outta here!"

RAP AS BIZ

Parker says that Run-D.M.C.'s forays into rock were fresh, and as novel as they were a novelty. However, he won't disagree that "Walk This Way" was as much a marketing move as an artistic one. "You're either going for the gold audience or the platinum audience," he remarks, "but usually those who go for the platinum audience will lose the respect of the core rap audience." Parker says some astute legal moves by his attorney in negotiations with RCA/Jive give him complete creative control over his productions, thus insulating him to a large degree from record company whims. Interestingly, rap has responded to the monolithic pop machine in the form of a loose cartel that presents a semblance of a unified front to the biz while allowing for enough rivalry to keep things lively. Parker sees the rap production world divided into three "families": his own Boogie Down productions, the estimable Def Jam and Cold Chillun'. But he says that, aside from the standards of good ol' American capitalism and survival of the economically fittest, they pull together under the philosophy that, "If we don't put rap out right, it's destroyed."

Can some uptown central committee set themselves up as arbiters of what's politically correct in an art form? "We have, and we have to," Parker replies. "The people who put out rap hits need to be in a positive setting and make it respectable."

Parker sees Def Jam (producers of Run-D.M.C.) as the most conservative of the rap operations. But rap, like rock, is renewing itself with an infusion of new blood. The latest comes from the West Coast: Delicious Vinyl, a homegrown, hometown, homeboy operation that has scored the biggest hit of all, Ton Loc's multiplatinum, Top 40 "Wild Thing." But its very success to Parker is an indication of a smudge on its purity. "Delicious Vinyl became very big, very fast, but they've already sold out to Island

"*Everyone is always hunting for the new boom. In the rap industry, not having an SP-12 [E-mu sampling drum machine] is like going to school with no books. Get outta here!*"

[Records], so now Island can become very big [in the rap field]. I'm still the only one that doesn't own its own label."

Rap is music of the ghetto, but Parker acknowledges that rap also exists in a parallel musical ghetto of sorts, as heavy metal once did. While the hardcore elements of both genres still reside in that ghetto with only the (large-budgeted) tips of the icebergs showing up in the mainstream, Parker says that country music might serve as a better analogy for rap's status. Both are music of class and economics rather than race and color. "There's such a thing as blacknecks as well as rednecks, you know," says Parker.

As a producer, Kris Parker isn't going to let things like the laws of acoustical and electrical physics, the orthodoxy of the record industry or time-honored production and engineering approaches get in the way of his personal Holy Grail—to get a jagged-edged, emotional reality into his records and, in the process, change the perception of an entire genre of contemporary music. "Rappers have a longer way to go because we have to knock off this negative image," concludes Parker. "Just getting past the party image is tough, let alone the violence thing. That's the reason for doing *Self Destruction*. I hope that a record that powerful will get played and cut through the emotional red tape. We want to give rap a better name."

▼▼▼

DANIEL LANOIS
Natural Focus

"*Too much polish on a record doesn't work for me anymore.*"

▼▼▼

BY IAIN BLAIR

"**W**HY'D IT TAKE me so long to finish *Acadia*? Because I kept getting sidetracked into doing other records I just couldn't say no to."

Daniel Lanois is sitting in an office at Warner Bros. Records, Burbank, talking about his debut album, which follows hot on the heels of the Neville Brothers' *Yellow Moon* and Bob Dylan's *Oh Mercy*, two of the projects the soft-spoken French-Canadian producer just couldn't say no to.

"I originally signed to Opal Records, Brian Eno's label, back in the beginning of 1988, and started some of the songs for *Acadia* down in New Orleans," Lanois says. "But then I bumped into the Neville Brothers and that was that. I *had* to produce their record. So I just stepped back from mine for a while, figuring I'd finish it up after the *Yellow Moon* sessions."

Lanois eventually got back to his own project, but only after agreeing to also produce Bob Dylan's album, again in New Orleans, where he had set up a studio in an old house. "I thought if I went down there to work, I'd be left undisturbed and get the album finished pretty quickly, but it didn't happen that way," he laughs. "But it all worked out for the best, because originally I had planned an instrumental record that was going to be very reflective and relatively quiet," Lanois reports. "After working with the Nevilles and Dylan, it turned into a vocal record with a much harder edge and, I hope, much stronger lyrics. They both inspired me to push myself."

The result is an eclectic, intriguing collection of 11 original songs (and a shimmering interpretation of "Amazing Grace") produced, naturally, by Lanois and featuring guest appearances from the likes of U2's Adam Clayton and Larry Mullen Jr., Brian and Roger Eno, the Neville Brothers and Mason Ruffner, among others.

As a producer and engineer, Lanois' musical portfolio is one of the most impressive in contemporary music. His credits range from albums for Peter Gabriel (*So*) and U2 (*The Unforgettable Fire*, *The Joshua Tree*) to Robbie Robertson's 1987 self-titled solo debut. Over the years, his musical vision has remained remarkably true to his original philosophy of recording: "Create a unique environment for each record wherever possible."

Born in Ottawa in 1951, Lanois began his recording career at an early age when, along with his brother Bob, he built his first studio in the family basement. "In the end we drove my mother crazy with the studio in her house, so we moved to a big house nearby in Hamilton, which became Grant Avenue Studio," he recalls. It was here that the Lanois brothers produced a string of hits for Canadian acts, including three albums for the Toronto-based band Martha and The Muffins (featuring his sister Jocelyn

on bass), for which Daniel was named Canada's Producer of the Year three years running.

These successes, which included pioneering aural explorations with Brian Eno, quickly led to the string of prestigious projects mentioned above.

▼▼▼

MIX: What music did you listen to in your teens? Who were your idols?
LANOIS: As a young guitarist, I was a big fan of Jimi Hendrix, Eric Clapton and Cream, but also more obscure people like Django Reinhardt and lots of jazz artists. But probably Hendrix and Clapton were the biggest influences.
MIX: How did you meet Brian Eno?
LANOIS: He heard a tape I'd done at Grant Avenue of a band called the Time Twins, who he met in New York. He really liked the sound, so he came to the studio to visit. I didn't know who he was; he just showed up and we started working on some ideas. He opened my eyes and showed me how to manipulate sound. In those days, engineers were very conventional in their approach to sessions. You recorded everything as dry and

flat as you could and then got everything right in the mix. But Brian had little respect for that philosophy—everything he did went to tape already manipulated and treated, and I thought that was an interesting approach. We had this way of using a 36-channel console, where channels 24 to 36 would be effects returns, and they'd be bused not into stereo but into two channels all the time, as if you were ready to print all those channels all the time. So at any given moment I could print the effects very quickly, and it seemed like an extreme idea, because at the time people only monitored effects. So if something sounded good with an effect, within two seconds I could get it down on tape. Technically speaking, that's the kind of thing we came up with.

MIX: Producing U2 was an important step for you. How did that happen?

LANOIS: It was through Brian. This was before the *Unforgettable Fire* record. They were interested in finding a new sonic direction for their sound, and they felt Brian Eno would be a good choice. Brian and I had been working together for a few years in Canada, and it seemed like a good idea to bring me along. That's how we met.

MIX: How did you hook up with Peter Gabriel?

LANOIS: Peter was looking to work with someone on a soundtrack for a film called *Birdy*, and he wanted to work with someone who was good at treating sound. He heard some of the work I did with Harold Budd, specifically *Plateaux of Mirror*, which we did with Brian Eno, and he just called me up.

MIX: Any interesting stories about the *So* sessions?

LANOIS: They were all pretty much sketched out first by Peter, myself and David Rhodes, and we had a strong house rule—we wouldn't rely on fixing things in the mix, but we'd try to capture a strong mood for each track using just the three of us and a rhythm box. Most of it was done in the control room at Peter's studio, and we hardly ever used earphones at all. We just used the monitors for the vocals. Even more unusual, most of the drums and bass tracks were overdubbed. I usually like to capture as much of the live playing as possible in any session, but these sessions were the reverse. It was sort of like overdubbing the rhythm section on top of a demo. That was the spirit of the record.

MIX: What about working with Robbie Robertson?

LANOIS: He operates in a very visual sense. He's loved films ever since he was a kid, and his writing is very visual. I like that a lot because I think the same way, and it's nice to share a philosophy with someone you're working with.

MIX: Let's talk a little about the Nevilles. What were you aiming for on *Yellow Moon*?

LANOIS: The main idea was to create a natural-sounding record and to let the band have a lot of input. They'd made a couple of records where the approach was largely dictated by the producers, and even the rhythm section had been excluded from some of that work, which is a real sin. That's the whole point of this band, so to make an album with a drum machine and ask the drummer to overdub is a mistake. I wanted to draw as much out of the band as possible, so I set up a portable studio in their neighborhood, brought in some portable equipment, and did the album in this old apartment house. It worked well because the whole focus was on them and the music.

MIX: What can you tell us about recording the Dylan album, *Oh Mercy*?

LANOIS: It took seven weeks to record, and we did it in a big house in uptown New Orleans. We took the house over, but mostly did everything in just one room, the control room. All the musicians set up there, including the drums. We only used the next room for the grand piano. It was a very intimate layout. I'd sit next to Bob, and Willie Green, the Nevilles' drummer, sat on the other side. So it was a tight little circle, and there's a kind of communication you get from being physically close that's hard to reproduce with cans or monitors.

MIX: What sort of equipment did you use?

LANOIS: I used a Studer A80 24-track with Dolby A—my favorite. A lot of it was cut at 15 ips, which I like because it gives you a great bass sound, really rich. On Bob's vocals, we used a Sony C-27A, a valve mic, through an LA-2A tube compressor, with a Neve 4-band preamp, a 1976 model, I think. So I went for the old sound in his voice and got a great, big, warm sound that also has a lot of presence. We punched that right into the patch bay, right to tape. The LA-2A has a volume control, an output level controller, so rather than use a fader, we just worked that control. I used a [TAC] Matchless console, which we used more for line returns than recording. For recording, we remained faithful to the outboard Neve system.

Essentially, we taped on Neve and then monitored and mixed through the Matchless.

MIX: Can you choose one track and break down the recording process in some detail?

LANOIS: Well, there was one song called "Most of the Time," which is powerful and textural, and we'd tried to lay it down with the full band and failed. The track just wasn't happening. So we then decided to go with a time reference using a Roland 808, but just the pulse. We played it in an intimate way, just Bob and I and Malcolm Byrne, the engineer, and overdubbed on top of this box two guitars and a keyboard and a vocal. It was very simple, and not unlike my approach to the *So* sessions with Peter Gabriel. Then I overdubbed the bass next, a hook-type response in the chorus, and then two Les Paul guitars, using my Les Paul Junior and a Vox AC30 cranked up all the way. It's a heavy guitar sound, but I set it away in the distance in the mix, so you just get this sense of power, but it's like a lid holding down the pressure. So in terms of aural perspective, the vocal is very much in the foreground and these power guitars are way off in the distance. Then, finally, Willie Green overdubbed the drums and Cyril Neville played percussion, so it was a kind of backward approach, but it's one of the most interesting tracks in terms of texture. There's a lot of anger bubbling under the surface.

MIX: How did you approach the mix?

LANOIS: That song was very difficult. We tried a lot of mixes, and Bob wasn't even sure the song should go on the album. But then one day I hit on the answer, which turned out to be a strange balance, but it worked the best. It ended up with the percussion being very upfront, and the drums are set back with a lot of echo. It's off-balance, but it works.

MIX: What about the mixes in general?

LANOIS: We had a policy of mixing at the end of every day, so if we did a vocal, we'd do a mix, and quite often that would end up being the final mix. The rough mix would capture what we wanted. We mixed everything to DAT, so if a rough mix turned out well, we had the quality.

MIX: How was it working with Dylan in the studio?

LANOIS: You know, he's an incredibly committed lyricist. I've never seen anyone work that hard on lyrics. He'd only work at night, starting around 8 p.m., and, of course, it got later and later as the record went on. By the end, he'd be arriving around midnight, and we'd go all night. Anyway, he had this fantastic concentration with the lyrics, and he'd come in with this page of words, and by the end of the night he'd have added on so much that this page would be a mass of graffiti that only he could decipher.

MIX: Tell us about your studio. Where is it?

LANOIS: It's currently in New Orleans, and it's basically a portable setup. Everything fits in cases, even the Studer A80, which is a giant machine. I just like the idea of being able to go anywhere and record. The console is really the main backbone, and the reason I use the Matchless is because I can carry it anywhere. Actually, since doing the Dylan album, I've bought the API console out of the Record Plant in New York. It's an early '70s model, one of the biggest APIs ever made, and I'm going to restore that in New Orleans in anticipation of having a more permanent studio in the future. It's essentially a private studio, although friends will call up and insist that they record there!

MIX: What other equipment do you have?

LANOIS: I use a Studer A80 1/2-inch, 2-track, 30 ips analog machine for edits. I mix to DAT, and if I need to do an edit on the spot, I'll transfer that to the 1/2-inch and do the edit. That works well. In fact, some things seem to improve with that extra generation. You get more of a mechanical sound and the bottom seems to improve.

As for the outboard gear, I use the big Lexicon reverb units, and I like Korg DDL-3000s—they're old favorites and I've got four of them. I prefer using them instead of direct boxes for instruments, because they've got a fantastic front-end amp. They sound better than any DI box I can think of. They also give me the opportunity to mess around a little with the sound if I want to print an effect. I use API outboard preamps and equalizers, 4-band and 3-band, four LA-2As and a pair of old Decca compressors, which have this great, warm sound I like for vocals. As for mics, I like the Sony C-37As. They have a really fat sound. I also use SM58s on some singers. For monitoring the musicians, I use earphones, but wherever possible I try to encourage the use of stage wedge monitors, so it's almost like a small P.A. system in the performance area, driven by heavy-duty Crest amps. As for the main monitors in the control room, I use a pair of old Tannoy Golds in Lockwood cabinets. To this day they're my favorites, and I've tried 'em all. I always come back.

MIX: Why do you like to record in unusual places?

LANOIS: Simply for the excitement. I like the idea of arriving somewhere new and transforming it into a studio. I like the strange rooms that you find in old houses and buildings. It gives you a sense of focus you just don't get when you're in a big complex. You get a sound that's unique to that record, a sonic signature, if you like.

MIX: Tell us about your solo album, *Acadia*.

LANOIS: Most of it was recorded at the same house in New Orleans where we did Dylan's album. In fact, after Bob's project, I just carried on with mine. It was the same equipment, same everything. But some of the record was done at Brian Eno's studio in England. He has a Harrison console and an MCI 24-track system. I spent two weeks there while he overdubbed some keyboards and did some background vocals. Again, it was the same working method, with everything being done in the control room. Then I moved to STS studio in Dublin, a little place that U2 uses for their demos, and as they were set up there at the time, I just moved in with my tapes, and Larry [Mullen] and Adam [Clayton] added some overdubs.

MIX: What was your overall approach?

LANOIS: The main thing I wanted to capture was a very natural-sounding record, like with the Nevilles. I also wanted a blend of acoustic sounds with electronic sounds. As you can hear on the record, there's a lot of breathing on my vocals, which is natural, and I didn't want to delete all that stuff. Similarly, if a feel was good but there was a little mistake on guitar, I'd just keep it. Too much polish on a record doesn't work for me anymore.

MIX: Any advice for kids starting out who want to be producers?

LANOIS: Get the most you can out of any given piece of equipment. If you like a certain sound, become a master at using it. From that will come a focus.

▼▼▼

BILL LASWELL
International
Enigma

*"**D**on't let judgment
get in the way of what
you hear."*

LASWELL IS AN instigator with good intentions, a catalyst with
good taste. He brings people together, sometimes from widely disparate backgrounds, throws them in a room and rolls the tape.
Friends drop by his private studio and jam; a fairly common practice among friends. But Laswell's friends happen to be Bootsy Collins,
Herbie Hancock, Ronald Shannon Jackson, George Clinton. Just get it
on tape, capture the energy and worry about the business details later,
that's Laswell's philosophy. The results vary, but sometimes there is magic
in the room. Laswell releases some of these miracles on his Axiom Records
label, a typically eclectic undertaking for the bassist-producer.

Laswell leaped into the public eye as a producer in 1983 with the release
of Herbie Hancock's *Future Shock*. The success of the high-tech-funk single
"Rock-It" kept Laswell's phone ringing for several years, leading to such
high-profile projects as Laurie Anderson's *Mr. Heartbreak* and Mick
Jagger's *She's The Boss*.

These days, Laswell seems less interested in high-tech and more intrigued by ethnic music, particularly the cross fertilization that occurs
when East meets West. Laswell continues to span the globe in search of
authentic sounds to document. Accompanied by a small crew of engineers,
he carries an Akai 12-track recorder with him on flights to Gambia, India,
Morocco and all throughout Asia.

Musician, producer, record company head—Laswell is all of these and
more. File him under enigma.

▼▼▼

BY BILL MILKOWSKI

▼▼▼

MIX: What is the thrust of Axiom Records?
LASWELL: It's a continuation of what my work has been through the
years [in the mid-'80s he formed OAO Records, an alternative music label
distributed by Celluloid Records], but now the label has another name.
MIX: Do you continue to do your thing?
LASWELL: Yeah, you have to. But a few things have changed for me.
There's more responsibility, because now there's a studio and a label. It's
not like a business, but it's definitely like balancing a community…it's deli-
cate and full of politics and subtlety.
MIX: You've expanded. Ten years ago, the community was pretty much

confined to downtown New York. Now it's international.

LASWELL: Well, there never really was a community in New York for me. People call what I was involved in Downtown music. All "Downtown" means is that people don't have enough money to get a better place to live. And when people start to make money, they get out of there, so then what they're doing is no longer considered Downtown. I don't have any affinity with being Downtown. I did a few records because I was getting started and that's where I lived, because I had no money. But you have to go on.

I've tried to branch out internationally, not just move out of the Village. I want to go everywhere and experience as much as possible, not as a tourist but as someone who's making real contact with people who are doing things musically. I want to document that music and present it more professionally and efficiently than it would be in a field recording.

MIX: I remember that when I talked to you in 1986, you were considering going into Japan and working with musicians there.

LASWELL: I ended up making something like 30 trips to Japan. From there I went more into Southeast Asia, to Thailand and Korea. I was especially intrigued by Okinawan pop music, which has some great guitar stuff. The *Neo Geo* project I did with Ryuichi Sakamoto was the beginning of that phase.

MIX: Do you feel the musical climate has changed at all since the Reagan years, that people at record companies are opening up to more challenging music?

LASWELL: I don't think people at record companies would know challenging music if it was right in their face. I've been hearing challenging things since I started listening to music. I've heard it in the streets, in the Middle East, in Africa, in India, in Asia. I've seen young kids who will go from listening to hardcore hip hop to skateboard thrash and hardcore music. That's a fusion that's inevitable and inspiring.

MIX: What are you particularly excited about?

LASWELL: Everything. Absolutely everything. There's a scene happening in Paris; there's a lot of young kids growing up in mixed neighborhoods— people from Africa, Martinique, the Middle East, all living together. These kids are growing up with rock music, hip hop, Moroccan music, the way we grew up with country & western, jazz and blues. For example, there's the French group I recorded, FFF. The singer is from Toga, the drummer's from Martinique, the rest are French. The music is a mixture of their different cultures—jazz, reggae, Caribbean—and yet they're totally devoted to James Brown and P-Funk. For the sessions, we brought T-Bone from Trouble Funk and Gary Mudbone Cooper from P-Funk, the

> "**I**f you have the right vibe and the right people, you can cut through any environment. You can create your own environment."

percussionist Ayib Deng from Gambia and all these guys. I guess in the end it'll be some kind of new take on funk.

MIX: So you're helping them realize their musical ideas?

LASWELL: Just getting them on tape, actually. Not really trying to educate them. What they're doing, they can't even discuss it intellectually. It's just natural growth. It's not like, "I need to get this book on West African drumming, then I'm going to go to the Asian Society and check out this, then I'm going to go and read about Harry Partch."

MIX: How did you find them?

LASWELL: They contacted me. I guess I have a reputation for being interested in that kind of stuff. And they love funk stuff. I did a record with these kids from San Francisco called The Limbomaniacs, and they liked that stuff. Plus, I was also associated with Bootsy and Maceo Parker and everybody. And they also knew of me from the fact that I worked previously in Paris on a lot of African stuff. I created a tremendous controversy over there awhile ago because I recorded all these African musicians with drum machines, and people were saying, "Oh, he's killing African music." I did a Manu Dibango record [*Electric Africa*], and there was also a Fela Kuti tape I remixed when he was in jail [*Army Arrangement*]. He played sax on this tape and I hated his playing, so I erased it and brought in Bernie Worrell to play organ instead. We got a lot of flak for that. Critics wrote that I was trying to destroy African music. But I can't see how that remotely compares to the other Fela records of that period. It's a much better record.

MIX: Have you been doing some field recording projects?

LASWELL: We just did this thing in India with [violinist] Shankar, which we recorded with eight or nine pieces in his home town in Madras. We found a studio there for $200 a day and we made it work. It really sounds good, which only goes to prove that you don't have to have a super high-tech studio with an SSL board to make your records sound good. It was a regular 24-track recording studio, and it did take a certain amount of manipulating whatever equipment was available. But Oz Fritz, my engineer, made it work with the equipment that was there. I also did these recordings in Morocco and West Africa with an Akai digital 12-track. Billy Youdelman, who is a master of field recording, engineered those sessions and the shit sounds better than a studio. There's one from Gambia that's recorded in a yard and it really sounds like something special.

MIX: So your ears are your main weapon.

LASWELL: Yeah, don't let judgment get in the way of what you can hear.

MIX: You mentioned this scene happening in Paris. Are there also pockets of creativity happening in the States now?

LASWELL: Oh yeah. All over the Midwest. For example, in Dayton, Ohio, and in Cincinnati, there are bands that are totally into skateboards and heavy metal on one side and hardcore hip hop on the other side. That's going to be a marriage of styles that's inevitable. And it's not for the marketplace, you know. It's more for people who want to hear it because they like it. It's coming out of a natural process…the environment is creating these situations.

MIX: What do you require of a studio? And what are your visions for the one you have?

LASWELL: Again, what we have is just a workspace, really. And that's probably what it's going to continue to be. But the idea is just to have a

place and use it for everything we need to do. It's not really set up for mixing. There's no automation, so we end up doing most of our mixing at Platinum Island in Manhattan. But the console here sounds great. It's an old Neve. And we've got a good 24-track Studer tape machine.

MIX: So you're not one of those guys who needs to have an SSL board.

LASWELL: I don't need anything. I just need a place to put some stuff, to try to get stuff happening. Mainly to get things on tape. And we have a facility now to do that.

MIX: So you haven't worked at the Power Station for a while?

LASWELL: I haven't worked there in maybe two or three years, really since I've been mixing at Platinum Island. I don't use a lot of different studios. I usually get stuck in a place for a year or two. In the early part of the '80s, I was at RPM a lot, then I got into working at Power Station and also a place called Quadrosonic, and Electric Ladyland a little bit. A lot of small studios too. I always preferred to do the live stuff in small places.

MIX: What does your room sound like?

LASWELL: It doesn't sound bad. All the drums and everything on this FFF record were done there. It's all about how you use a room. People have these misconceptions: get a giant room, get a big drum sound. A lot of the biggest-sounding drums have been recorded in tiny rooms. It's about cranking the mic and recording ambience.

MIX: Like how you got that huge drum sound on the Public Image Ltd. project by recording the drums in an elevator shaft at the Power Station.

LASWELL: Yeah, stuff like that. That's obviously a very small room, but it's a huge sound. But I think we can gradually make my studio into a lot of different sounding rooms.

MIX: I didn't notice much sonex or baffling.

LASWELL: There isn't much, but I can create houses and enclosures with foam rubber. You take an amp like a Marshall and just completely cover it in foam rubber. We got the idea for that from Sorcerer Sound. Al Fierstein bought all this foam rubber on Canal Street, so he could record a live band with drums right in the room and all the amps and he'd have very little leakage from the drums. It's great for cutting basics. I've done that many times. Then if you want a more open guitar sound, you have to do that as an overdub because you're going to have to back up and get a room mic. But if you just want the basic sound coming out of the speaker right into the mic, you can put it in a house like that and you won't have leakage from the drums. That way you don't have to separate the drummer in a booth, because the room sounds good live.

*F*riends drop by his private studio and jam; a fairly common practice among friends. But Laswell's friends happen to be Bootsy Collins, Herbie Hancock, Ronald Shannon Jackson, George Clinton.

MIX: You seem to have tons of master tape lying around your studio.

LASWELL: There are a lot of projects that were not defined as to what they were. Sometimes somebody might be coming through town, and we'll record something and save it. There are people who travel a lot and might not come back for a year. And you might want to have them on tape for something else, totally.

MIX: That's a cool way to do it. There's so many high-tech studios around with clinical environments, like a hospital or something. It doesn't seem to be about music, more about commerce.

LASWELL: It's not about music at all. Even slightly. I don't know what it's about, to be honest with you. There's probably a kind of music that is perfect for that environment, but I can't imagine what it would sound like, or who would be playing it and why. I don't work in those kind of studios. If you have the right vibe and right people, you can cut through any environment. You can create your own environment, but I think you need a gang of people to do it. What we have here feels good; it's a raw space, and a lot of work's getting done.

MIX: Over the last ten years, have you developed technical chops in the studio in terms of, say, miking techniques?

LASWELL: I usually have an idea of what I want to do sonically. I have preferences in terms of all the instruments, but I'm open to someone making it sound better than I could've imagined. And that happens quite a lot. I think that's because I'm working with the right people and giving them enough freedom to be creative. You could have anybody in there putting the stuff up and doing what you're saying. There's no sense really in having relationships with engineers; people ought to have the space to be creative. I like to get everything on tape a certain way, the way I like to hear it. And it's not really based on any repetitive techniques, just the way it sounds. I know what the instruments sound like, I know that if you put them through this effect or EQ it a certain way it'll sound that way every time. So repeating techniques does happen on occasion. But sometimes it's an accident that makes things sound better than you could've imagined.

MIX: So you haven't evolved any formulas for miking techniques?

LASWELL: Every one has their own techniques, but there's not a lot to miking something. You need a good mic and a good console and a tape machine, but more than that you need to get somebody who's going to record something and make it sound real. Youdelman, the guy who does field recording, has a good ear for what instruments sound like. So he can listen to an instrument and know where the sound is coming from and how to get it on tape. Listening and really hearing is something that a lot of people don't participate in. They're too caught up in other activity, like talking about something or being influenced by some cut they heard somebody else do. There are very few people who are actually listening.

▼▼▼

TOM LORD-ALGE
The Grammy-Winning Producer Is on a Roll

"**I**'M ONE OF a new breed of engineers," Tom Lord-Alge says with characteristic confidence as he sits in a lounge at San Francisco's Different Fur Recording. "The new breed is willing to go for it, do whatever it takes to make a great record. They're not afraid to use EQ. They're not afraid to use compression. They'll take control of a session even if they're not producing. They're not timid. They do whatever it takes to make it sound different, less predictable—like totally whacking things out of perspective. It's a little like hot-rod mixing."

This could just be bold talk from some young turk, except that Lord-Alge has the credentials to back it up. He's won two Grammys for engineering, and over the past few years he's become a real triple threat—in demand for his producing, engineering and mixing skills. He still has the fire of youth burning inside, with a self-assurance that borders on arrogance at times and enough energy to wear out the heartiest artist (or interviewer, for that matter). I wasn't surprised to learn he's from New Jersey.

"There was always music in the house," Lord-Alge says of his youth. No wonder: his mother is a jazz pianist of some note (Vivian Lord), and his father was in the jukebox business. Unlike his older brothers Jeff and Chris, Tom didn't play music. Instead, he spent his late teen years doing live sound for his brothers' (and other) bands. "I did it all," he says. "I'd hump the gear, drive the truck, load the P.A., set up the mics and mix the shows." Eventually he became successful enough that he had roadies do some of those tasks.

One New Year's Eve, though, "I got in a fight with the band I was working for. They fired me, so I took all my gear and left them high and dry without a P.A. on New Year's," he says with a sadistic chuckle. "The day after New Year's, I started working with my brother Chris as an assistant engineer. I did that for two months and then started engineering my own sessions."

His rise since then has been steady and fairly rapid. Lord-Alge cut his teeth mainly at Unique Recording in Manhattan, working on a broad vari-

"*I'm not a musician, but the SSL is my instrument.*"

▼▼▼

BY BLAIR JACKSON

ety of engineering and mixing projects, and eventually got into production as well. Though he is best known for engineering the records that earned him his Grammys—Steve Winwood's *Back in the High Life* and *Roll With It* (which he also co-produced)—mixing is still his greatest passion. In that capacity alone, he's worked on songs by Toni Childs, Spandau Ballet, Belinda Carlisle, Peter Gabriel (the superb "Big Time" 12-inch), Billy Idol and others.

I caught up with Lord-Alge at Different Fur as he prepared for another day of sessions with Starship, for whom he produced six tracks. "They're great players, and Mickey Thomas has an amazing voice," he says. "This record has more of a big R&B feel on the tracks, which is what I do best. I think people may be surprised by this record. I know I'm enjoying it."

As you'll see, this is one enthusiastic guy.

▼▼▼

MIX: Did you have any impression of what studio life was like before you got involved with it?
LORD-ALGE: No, not at all. When I first started engineering, I wondered, "Well, what's the trick here? You can rewind!" Obviously I wasn't doing great mixes, but I would have a mix up before a four-minute song was over because I was so used to mixing fast from working in live sound. Half the time when I was doing live sound, we wouldn't have a soundcheck, so I'd have to do everything—a mix and effects—during the first couple of minutes of the first tune. Obviously, as I did more engineering, I took more time, but I still work fast.

I'm not a musician, but I'm a listener, so I knew how to hear how a mix should sound, how it should be balanced. Chris [his brother] taught me the physical end of it—the routing, how to deal with effects, how to bounce, that sort of thing. He was a great teacher, and I was able to pick things up pretty quickly.
MIX: You went from being an assistant to engineering sessions on your own. What was that transition like?
LORD-ALGE: Chris had no mercy on me. [Laughs] He threw me into everything he could. I was petrified at first, but that's one way to learn. We'd be in the middle of cutting vocals and Chris would just leave the room; if I wasn't totally on top of it, we were in trouble. That's one of the things he instilled in me—that an assistant should always be right on top of everything that's going on. I don't think that's usually the case these days, though I've worked with many fine assistants.

He kept throwing me in the hot seat, and I had to either perform and do it well or I'd have to go look for another gig. I also assisted some of the other staff engineers at Unique, and sometimes when they'd leave the room I'd do my thing right in front of the client and basically rob the client away. [Laughs]

Chris is really the person most responsible for what I'm doing today. I can't say enough about that. Sometimes I wish it was he who won the Grammy, because he really deserves it. I think he's a better engineer than me, although it's hard to compare because we have different tastes and mix differently.
MIX: Can you remember the first time you felt like you made a real contribution to how a record sounded?
LORD-ALGE: Probably Orchestral Manoeuvres in the Dark's "If You

> "**I** record with the mix in mind."

Leave," which was the first record I ever produced. It made it to Number Four.

That came about through Chris, too. Way before "If You Leave," OMD wanted Chris to do a 12-inch of one of their songs, but he was sick that day, so he sent me in. I explained who I was and what the situation was, and they only had a day in New York, so they gave it a go. It worked out well enough that a couple of months later they asked me to go out to L.A. to produce a song for the soundtrack of *Pretty in Pink*. We recorded it over three days at Larrabee, mixed it the fourth day, and it did great. It was a very exciting way to break into production.

MIX: Isn't it hard to get into a rhythm when you're only cutting one or two songs with a band?

LORD-ALGE: It depends on whether you're producing it or just mixing it. Mixing is cake. I can do as many or as few songs as they want.

MIX: What is your responsibility as a mixer on a 12-inch? How are you trying to serve the song?

LORD-ALGE: I'm trying to f— it up as much as I can! [Laughs] I'm extending it, putting breaks in it. I overdub parts on it, maybe change the bass line, add percussion, tear the choruses apart.

It's a cool thing and I started out doing it, but it's not really what I'm into right now. I'll do it, but only if I get the single, too, because that's where my talent lies.

MIX: What do you think is the key to a good mix?

LORD-ALGE: A good performance. If it ain't on tape, you're just polishing a turd. I try hard to get a great vocal performance, because so much of how a song works is based on the vocal. I learned a lot working with Steve [Winwood], who is obviously a great singer.

MIX: Can you talk a little about working with Winwood? It must have been interesting to go into the studio with someone who has made so many records through the years, and who obviously knows what he wants in the studio by now.

LORD-ALGE: He's also engineered and mixed some of his albums, so

when I first started working with Steve I was very, very nervous. I grew up listening to his music. I wasn't a huge Traffic fan, but I liked them and I knew their music. I loved Blind Faith, and I've liked some of his solo albums. Who couldn't like *Arc of a Diver*? It was a brilliant record.

I originally got involved with Steve through a good friend of mine who I'm forever indebted to, Robbie Kilgore. Robbie is one of my favorite New York session keyboard players. He comes up with these incredible, off-the-wall, wacky keyboard parts. Anyway, he was programming keyboards for Steve on the *Back in the High Life* album, and I was still on staff at Unique. Robbie had recommended that they go to Unique because the studio had all the latest technology and these hot young engineers. So they did end up at Unique and we hit it off.

MIX: What stage was the album in at that point?

LORD-ALGE: They had just cut basic tracks with Jason Corsaro, who's a good friend of mine at Power Station. Drum machine, synth bass, some vocals—everything was in its basic form.

Maybe ten to twenty percent of what was on the tapes when I started working on it, stayed on it. We redid a lot of it—vocals, some bass parts—and we put on live drums. I worked on that record for eight months. Working with Steve was amazing. We had a great time.

He really knows his way around the studio; he even taught me some things about the SSL I didn't know. He owned one of the first SSLs at his home studio when they came out years ago. In turn, I taught him some things about the SSL, which was cool. I'm not a musician, but the SSL is my instrument.

MIX: How did the experience of making *Roll With It* compare with *Back in the High Life*?

LORD-ALGE: It was much easier all the way around. For one thing, I produced *Roll With It*, whereas Russ Titelman worked on *Back in the High Life*. But it was also the difference between spending eight months on something, and only 15 weeks, which is how long *Roll With It* took from blank tape to final mix. We didn't want to spend a lot of time mulling everything over. We wanted to come up with great performances and get them on tape. Steve had the songs already written, which is always a big help, and then he got the majority of the vocals on the first take. He works well that way, because on that first take he's not thinking, he's just singing.

MIX: Did you and Steve feel any pressure to try to follow up *Back in the High Life*?

LORD-ALGE: Nope. We were very comfortable. We never felt like we had to put out a certain kind of record. We didn't think we had to come out with *Back in the High Life, Part Two*, and I don't think we did. This record shows a different side of Steve. We went back to the roots with "Roll With It." Yeah, that's real close to some other songs, but that's Winwood, man. Those other songs are Winwood. We had the Hammond organ and piano and live drums, the Memphis Horns—that's Steve. We had a lot of fun with that song.

MIX: Do you have a regimen in the studio? Are there certain ways you like to approach a project?

LORD-ALGE: How I like to work when I'm producing and cutting basic tracks is—depending on the song—first, program it with a drum machine and a sequencer, or a Fairlight or whatever. Program the basic parts—drums, a bass line, a couple of keyboard pads—into the computer, and then manipulate the arrangement to make it as good as possible. When you do it that way, it's easier to hear how you might change things. You can say, "Let's move this here, and we'll add a few beats there. Take this bar out." When that's done I'll print it, put a guide vocal down, lay some other parts down. Then what I've been doing—like with *High Life* and *Roll With It*—is to overdub a lot of things to the drum machine track and then, as you get to the end of the album, bring in the live drums to get that human feel, to swing it a little. John Robinson, who we worked with on those records, worked out perfectly. He's phenomenal. Steve played the drums on "Roll With It."

MIX: You've done a lot of your work at The Hit Factory [in Manhattan]. What is it about the studio that you like so much?

LORD-ALGE: I feel comfortable there. The rooms are good, there are no disruptions and everything works. The monitors sound good and everything is set up nicely. It's a sterling studio. But I like any studio that runs efficiently. I get upset when I'm in a studio and stuff doesn't work. I can't tolerate maintenance problems. Studios can't have shoddy maintenance and expect business.

MIX: You seem like an intense guy. Are you demanding of the artists you work with?

LORD-ALGE: I'm demanding, sure. I guess I have a pretty strong personality in the control room. There are certain things I like to hear, and I know how to get the sound I want. I'll tell an artist if I disagree and why. At the same time, though, it's not just my session. I try to keep the vibe happening. I don't put pressure on the artist. I'm flexible. Usually, when I have musicians come in, I let them do their thing and see what they want to play for a part, because you usually get a better performance than if you're just telling them what you want.

Always have the machine in "record." That's my motto. You get some of the best stuff that way. As long as you have an open track, keep it in "record." We're in the recording business! Any time there are musicians in there screwing around, or singers warming up, or whatever, you should be recording. 'Cause if it ain't on tape, it ain't there.

MIX: Have you had happy accidents that way?

LORD-ALGE: All the time. Every record. Yesterday we had one. Someone was just fooling around and came up with a great part. And we got it on tape.

Do you know the song "Valerie" on [Winwood's] *Chronicles*? The intro starts out with a tom fill, which is cool, and it's something nobody would play if they sat down and thought about it. How that came about was that I had just rewound the tape. I put it in "record" automatically, and Steve was messing around on drums; not playing in time or anything. Well, he played a fill that turned out to be absolutely perfect for the song. He didn't even know I was rolling.

MIX: When you're producing a track, at what point do you start thinking about effects?

LORD-ALGE: From the beginning. I record with the mix in mind. The less I have to do in the mix, the better. I put the effects on the tape, and then maybe I'll put even more on later. I'll print reverb—whatever I have to do

"*Always have the machine in 'record.' You get some of the best stuff that way. Any time there are musicians in there screwing around, or singers warming up, you should be recording. 'Cause if it ain't on tape, it ain't there.*"

to make it sound good.

MIX: Do you have favorite effects—some starting point?

LORD-ALGE: The Publison Infernal Machine 90 is one of my favorites. My all-time favorite reverb is probably the Sony DRE-2000. It's very natural, great on drums, great on creating a room. I'd like to think that my brother Chris and I had something to do with reviving the DRE-2000 somewhat, because they're starting to turn up at more and more studios, where before we could almost never find them.

I like using rooms and chambers. I'll use anything—greenhouses, hallways.

MIX: Greenhouses?

LORD-ALGE: Steve's house has a greenhouse. We've recorded drums in there, and it sounds very interesting.

MIX: You're a real advocate of the SSL console. Do you think that'll be the case for some years to come?

LORD-ALGE: Absolutely. I think SSL is sitting very pretty. It's weird—a lot of people who like Neve don't like SSL and people who like SSL don't like Neve. I like Neves, particularly the old ones, which sound great. But you can get any sound you want out of an SSL.

MIX: You've done a lot of digital recording, haven't you?

LORD-ALGE: Sure. *Roll With It* was digital. I think the Spandau Ballet album I mixed was the first session on the new 48-track digital Sony machine. They did it on two 3324s, then I took the master tape and transferred the slave onto the other 24 tracks. Brilliant machine.

MIX: Has it spoiled you?

LORD-ALGE: Absolutely. [Laughs] I don't ever want to mix an album with two tapes again—but I will, of course. You're just running one tape, and you don't have to wait for lockup—incredible! The Hit Factory has two of them.

I prefer recording digitally. I actually prefer the Mitsubishi system, because to my hearing it has a bit of a bump on the bottom end that I like. It sounds like analog tape without the hiss.

MIX: Have you worked with Dolby SR?

LORD-ALGE: I mixed a Billy Idol record that was recorded with SR, and I thought it sounded great. Personally, I'm really into mixing digital, though I've had a lot of people tell me I should try mixing to 1/2-inch Dolby SR. I think on this album [the Starship record] I'll try Dolby SR and run DAT. I usually mix right to Sony Pro DAT at 44.1 and then dump it to 1630 and do my edits. I love the way it sounds.

MIX: How do you avoid becoming predictable in your work?

LORD-ALGE: I just keep looking for new things. Maybe I avoid it by coming into the studio each morning and putting Def Leppard on "10" and blowing my brains out. [Laughs] Actually, I did that while I was working on *Roll With It*. I think *Hysteria* is the best rock 'n' roll record to come out since Led Zeppelin. One week I'd listen to "Pour Some Sugar On Me" every morning while I had my coffee—sit at the console with my coffee and put it up to "10" on the big speakers. The next week I'd play "Armageddon" every morning. So after that I'd be like, "Yeeaaaahhh!" I'd be pumped up and ready to work. In fact, you couldn't stop me if you wanted to. That's one way to do it. [Laughs]

▼▼▼

JEFF LYNNE
Lightens Up

Since 1987 when, without much fanfare, he produced some songs on a Duane Eddy album for Capitol, Jeff Lynne has gradually turned his old job of Electric Light Orchestra leader into his current position as superstar rock producer. Following Eddy, the clients have been enormous, often legendary names: George Harrison, Brian Wilson, Randy Newman, Tom Petty, the late Roy Orbison and Del Shannon. And, with Orbison, Petty, Bob Dylan and Harrison, he teamed up for the albums that made him a Traveling Wilbury.

His solo album, *Armchair Theatre*, was named after an old TV show that ran in his native Britain. Recorded in the studio he had installed in his sprawling 15th century home in England, the album contains rockers and ballads, a couple of pop standards ("September Song" and "Stormy Weather") and a transcontinental lament featuring Indian vocalists from Ravi Shankar's group.

In this interview, Lynne talks about *Armchair Theatre* and some of the principles that have guided his productions.

▼▼▼

MIX: When you were growing up, were you obsessed by particular pop records? The Beatles, maybe? The Beach Boys?
LYNNE: That's funny. I wasn't going to mention them. I think the first records that inspired me to want to do music were Del Shannon's. I also loved Roy Orbison, for a different reason. I think some of Orbison's recordings are still among the best pop records ever made.
MIX: Do you think of Orbison's singles as examples of vocal-centered productions?
LYNNE: Obviously, the vocal was very important. I've since learned from Roy and from Del—as I recorded both of them—what the techniques were. It's quite amazing. They told me that they recorded Orbison on three tracks, that there would be three discrete channels, and that there would be three speakers as well. So they'd have the strings coming out of one speaker, the voice coming out of the other and the backing track out of the other. It was like a three-way stereo system.
MIX: But those recordings remain models for you, correct?
LYNNE: Those recordings—the atmosphere, the sound! I just can't account for the skill of the session guys who used to play them. If it was exactly as they tell me, they'd just walk in, learn the songs, have a three-hour session and do it. [I don't know] how they thought of all those fantastic riffs and brilliant drum breaks in that short period of time. They must have been of a much higher standard than we are today.

> **"The sound of a room is much nicer to me than the sound of a gadget."**

▼▼▼

BY JAMES HUNTER

We're spoiled because we've got 24 tracks, or more, and we can keep second-guessing forever, which can be a bad thing. It's nice to have the luxury, but sometimes you lose track of what you're doing, because you keep fiddling about so much, mainly because you're able to.

MIX: Maybe '50s and '60s session musicians were hungrier, better able to capitalize on the limited time they had.

LYNNE: I guess so, but it also tells you where the priorities were, because if they were making million-selling records, then given three hours to record—how much could it have cost? It seems a bit daft that everyone was making fortunes, and yet in the studio you could only spend three hours. George Harrison has a nice line about sessions of that era: "Yeah, the first album took eight hours to make, and the next one took even longer."

MIX: Do you hear a so-called "Jeff Lynne sound" on your recordings?

LYNNE: Yeah, I do, actually, because people keep telling me there is one, so I've come to believe it. I do have a sound and I know what it is, but I can't explain it.

MIX: It seems really live on the one hand, highly crafted on the other.

LYNNE: I have to spend days making it sound like it was done in minutes. I mike things so that some parts sound live; other parts *are* live. I'm trying to create out of the same set of values that informed a record from the '60s, with people knowing what they're doing and being good at it, even though I don't think people can really do it anymore like the old guys did. But on the other hand, you get the later Beatles stuff, for example, which took a year to make and is brilliant.

THE TRAVELING WILBURYS' SECOND INCARNATION (LEFT TO RIGHT): JEFF LYNNE, BOB DYLAN, TOM PETTY AND GEORGE HARRISON

MIX: People associate a certain looseness with the Traveling Wilburys and Tom Petty's *Full Moon Fever*. Did you intend a similar feel for *Armchair Theatre*?

LYNNE: Well, Tom's record was done in a second. When I met with him to do it, he'd heard George's *Cloud Nine* album and he really liked the sound of that. He said, "Would you fancy writing a song together and see what we come up with?" So we came up with "Free Fallin'" in Mike Campbell's garage, and we recorded it there. I didn't treat Tom's album as I'd normally treat a project. We did the track, I went home and worked out all the parts for the guitar, keyboards, everything. And I always play bass if I'm producing someone—it's in the fine print—just kidding. But then when we finished it, we said, "Well, that was fun. Let's do another one." So we finished that song and mixed it. The whole album went like that: "Well, let's do another one." I ended up doing the whole lot. Usually, I would be working on ten songs at once.

MIX: And being more hands-on about it?

LYNNE: Well, hands-on in the arrangements, yeah. I like to play a lot of things if I'm producing. I like to do my homework. I like to take home a rough mix, and I like to try to develop parts so that when I come 'round the next day I can say, "How about this?" You don't have to sit and agonize over the parts while we're all sitting around doing them.

MIX: Which, in your view, is a waste of time.

LYNNE: Absolutely. I like to have things to play. I like to see if they work.

MIX: When you did *Armchair Theatre*, did you follow your recent thinking about the importance of vocals up in the mix?

LYNNE: I wanted to get the vocals real dry and up there, like I did on Tom's album, because Tom's got a great voice, and I think in the past he's always been sort of swamped in reverb and stuff. I'm not a fan of reverb at all. I spend a lot of time putting the mic in different places, because the sound of a room is much nicer to me than the sound of a gadget. I love the intimacy of a dry vocal up front.

MIX: Dimensionality improves.

LYNNE: You can almost picture it. The singer is right there in front of the band in the middle, then the instruments are where they should be. That's what I try to get, anyway.

MIX: A rock bias against recording vocals clearly seems to have asserted itself over the years. Maybe it was because the Rolling Stones' recordings did such great stuff with murk.

LYNNE: There was a lot of reverb there. I went through it with ELO records—I mixed myself right down, with echo—not reverb, particularly, but all gadgets, ADT and all that. But that's insecurity and hiding, that's all. I've lately gotten into the thing of, "Well, if he's singing it, we might as well hear it. Otherwise, don't bother." I've really taken a lot of care over the past years with miking. And Richard Dodd, my engineer, is a great one. He takes absolute care over stuff like that. We don't actually have to spend much time. It's strategic.

MIX: Do you have some techniques you favor over others?

LYNNE: It's evolving all the time. There are certain things I like to do. For example, I only use a couple of tracks for miking drums, ever. I see sessions where there are 17 drum tracks and three machines locked together. I like to get it all on 24 tracks. If I can't get it all on that, I shouldn't bother.

MIX: But didn't you do that sort of thing with later ELO material? Do you now view that music as fairly left-field?

LYNNE: Yeah, some of the stuff seems amazingly left-field when I hear it now. And I wonder, what was I thinking? I said I was the group's producer, and they said, "Oh, okay." And as we all know, you've got to learn to be a producer. But some of my early ideas were good, and a bit wacky and bold. And then I learned more and more as I went on, and I made some real pop records, proper ones that were within the scope of the pop-rock mainstream. But I probably messed up a few of those recordings by burying the voice too low.

MIX: Your work, in some ways, is simpler now.

LYNNE: People always thought that ELO was so complex. Actually, it was just a lot of very simple parts all put together. It's a bit like a jigsaw puzzle. But what I've tried to do more recently is thin it down and make it more like a small group than an enormous one. Although I've tried to leave it sounding big.

I've learned a lot of basic things, things that are so simple that I may have overlooked them in the past. I feel really good about making records

"People always thought that ELO was so complex. Actually, it was just a lot of very simple parts all put together. It's a bit like a jigsaw puzzle."

again. I went through a period where I wasn't enjoying it, where I started getting into digital sequencers and all that stuff, typing numbers in, which I hated. What I'm referring to is the later ELO albums, where I was dabbling in all this gear. So, when George Harrison called me to do his album, we both said how much we didn't like playing at computer operators, and how much we really liked to play. So we played everything by hand and had fun. And since that album, all the stuff I've done has been done by hand.

MIX: Why a solo album now?

LYNNE: Because Warner Bros. asked me if I'd like to make an album for them. At the end of ELO, I didn't know what I wanted to do. I was still playing about in my little studio—I used to have a small one upstairs—and I used to make up songs and demos for my own fun. But I never realized that I wanted to be a producer. Well, I sort of did, but having gone through the experience of all that digital stuff, I'd gone off it a bit. And then while I was working on *Cloud Nine*, Warner asked me if I'd like to do an album for myself.

But it took me all this time, because I did the Wilburys, Tom's album and parts of Roy's album. As soon as I had some clear time, I booked my engineer for six or seven months. We built the studio in two days with the help of a little company in England called Raindirk. And I got a desk from Cyril Jones, Raindirk's owner. He made a lovely 40-channel desk, with really nice EQ—not that we have to use it much, because we put the mics in the right place.

MIX: *Armchair Theatre* puts you center stage. Are you at home there?

LYNNE: Before, I liked hiding more. I mean, I'm still not a performer in the sense of a showman. But I just love making records. So to make my own record was an absolute pleasure, because there were a lot of musical statements that I wanted to make, and I wanted to make them without being under any constraints.

MIX: Your vocals are up front now.

LYNNE: I'm more confident now just singing and not being such a drama queen. I'm still a bit picky with my own vocals, but in fact there are a few tracks on *Armchair Theatre* where I've sung all the way through in one take. Before, on ELO tracks, I would never even sing until the backing track was finished, with a 40-piece orchestra and a whole chorus and everything on it. And nobody ever knew what the tune was except me. And I would save it, because I was embarrassed to sing it at first. Now I put rough vocals on things. I don't worry as much.

MIX: Do you want to be a star?

LYNNE: I'm a record maker, and I'm a singer. But I don't particularly want to be on TV every day.

▼▼▼

BRIAN MALOUF
Musical Chameleon

"**A** LOT OF PEOPLE are very specific about the kind of music they want to work on and be associated with," says producer/ engineer Brian Malouf. "I'm not putting that down. I've just never been the kind of person who has been able to resist anything that I think is good in its own genre."

Music, like many fields, has its share of specialists. These people, for better or worse, get associated with one type of music — Ron Nevison for hard rock, L.A. Reid for dance, Jimmy Bowen for country — and that becomes what they do. But what happens when an artist decides to do something out of character, either with one track or an entire project? As more artists explore different sounds, the times may once again be ripe for musical chameleons.

"My musical tastes have been eclectic all my life," Malouf says. "That lack of snobbery helps and hurts. When I was growing up as a musician, I always loved Top 40 radio. It didn't matter much to me if they were R&B or rock 'n' roll or any of the different styles I've worked on in my recording career. So long as it's good music and it's played well, I understand it. Because I understand it, I can put it across. That's why I've been so diverse. I want to keep it that way."

Brian Malouf is looking for diversity on any number of fronts. He's worked on a wide range of projects including cutting basic tracks with Michael Jackson, producing for Keedy and Australian rockers Pseudo Echo, mixing for rockers Slaughter and engineering the Madonna album *I'm Breathless* and soundtrack music for the film *Dick Tracy*.

"Right now, if I had my druthers," he says, "I would sit and record live tracking dates half the time, mix half the time and produce half the time. I'd have three halves to my life. I'd be really happy."

With the Madonna record, he got to dabble in the big band genre, a type of music he hadn't worked with since the Manhattan Transfer's *Vocalese*, when he recorded three tracks with the Count Basie Band.

"The Madonna stuff was sort of a hybrid," he remarks. "She and Pat [Leonard, producer] work fast. Everything they do becomes a master, even though it starts out as a songwriting session or a demo of a song that they have been working on. Those tracks were done at his studio, starting with Madonna and him singing and an Akai-Linn drum machine. We

"*I don't add things until they cry to be added.*"

▼▼▼
BY HANK BORDOWITZ

65
Brian Malouf

would go in with something like a MIDI track and vocal, and overdub the big band to that. Drummer Jeff Porcaro played in a big iso room and the rest of the band was out on the floor. They would perform over what we had already done. Madonna also wanted it to be somewhat electric, so as not to abandon everything she had done before."

Of course, recording a '40s-style big band in a contemporary pop context is not without its challenges. For example, do you track all the parts simultaneously? If you are using a string section, that means cramming 30 people into a studio, miking them and, for all intents and purposes, mixing them live.

"On two of the songs it was all together," Malouf recalls, "but on two others it was separate. For the bigger string section, it was kind of crowded. There were also some things with a smaller string section. We did one tune that actually turned out to be a duet with Warren Beatty, which was more like a speakeasy. There were maybe seven strings and four brass and woodwinds."

On working with Madonna, Malouf says, "She can cram more into six hours in the studio than most people can get into a week. She's exhilarating to work with—dynamic, challenging. A lot of people have trouble with that—they don't like being challenged as much. Being in the studio with her was one of the most fun times I've ever had. We got along well, and I love Pat Leonard, too. He's always fun to work with. We did that whole record in about six weeks. It went so fast."

Malouf had worked in this genre as a musician also, playing drums in his high school big band. "I've been a drummer since I was nine years old," he notes. "In high school, I floundered around, dabbled in bass and guitar, a couple of brass instruments, trombone and baritone horn. But I got tired of counting rests, which you do a lot in orchestra, and started playing drums again. In college, I settled into percussion. I spent five years really hitting it hard. That's when I analyzed Top 40 music. I was doing arrangements for my band. Then I developed arthritis in my knees. I was playing during the disco era, and I went through both knees. I turned the drum set around after my right knee went out and played left-handed until my left knee went out. It was after that band that I started engineering."

Malouf landed an apprenticeship at El Dorado Studios in Hollywood and from there moved to Can Am, where most of the projects he's been associated with were recorded. He currently holds the title of chief engineer. That position has taken him all over the map musically, from Madonna to Slaughter.

"I can't think of anything fundamentally different that I would do with either kind of music," he explains. "I approach both the same way as I would anything else—that is, throw up all the faders in a roughly straight line and listen to what is coming off the tape. Let that dictate all my moves. I'll figure out what kind of ambience I want, what kind of placement the vocals should be in, etc.

"The main thing about a record like Slaughter's is how the drums are going to sound, because that is what determines the attitude of the record. I don't add things until they cry to be added, as far as processing is concerned."

Although Malouf still primarily works as an engineer and remixer, he has set his sights on doing more actual production, and the projects are starting to fall his way. That's what working on a few name projects can do.

"Because I've worked on so many albums as an engineer," Malouf says, "I've got a good sense of how records are made. As a producer, I try to rely on my experience as a musician to get through the sessions: who to hire, what to play. I can write out charts and things like that. Most of what I know as an engineer I can also apply to producing, too. Of course, when you produce you're getting involved earlier in the project—listening to the demos and paying close attention to the performances and not just the sound.

"I enjoy producing because it gives you the feeling of *making* the record, not just mixing it. But I hope I never have to give up mixing, either."

▼▼▼

"So long as it's good music and it's played well, I understand it. Because I understand it, I can put it across."

GEORGE MARTIN & JOHN BURGESS
High Tea

"*I think the sound of a natural instrument is the best. All this technology and eternal synthesized sound and programming and mechanics is making music a bit sterile.*"
— *George Martin*

▼▼▼

BY MR. BONZAI

IN 1967, AT age 20, I sailed for Europe with a scholarship to study at the University of Edinburgh, Scotland. The funding allowed me to pursue my real goal—to meet John Lennon. Through inspired persistence and good fortune, I was invited into his home and he took me along to my first recording session. It was "I Am the Walrus," Abbey Road, and an evening that led me to become an engineer, disc jockey and chronicler of the music industry.

After more than two decades, I met with George Martin again, who was joined by his longtime friend and partner, John Burgess. They both started their careers at EMI, when records were 78s and tape recording was not yet part of the business. After nearly four decades in the studio, they are still as active as ever and offer some provocative thoughts about this funny business of making music.

▼▼▼

BONZAI: Early in your career you produced hundreds of comedy records, music hall-style songs.
MARTIN: Yes, I did a lot of spoken word records, a lot of musicals. I did children's records, and all of the Peter Sellers records, and worked with Beyond the Fringe—Jonathan Miller, Dudley Moore, Allen Bennet. I also produced the team of Flanders & Swann, which was a mixture of speech and music. In those days—this was pre-Beatles—I became known as a producer of funny records.
BONZAI: I've read your hilarious descriptions of getting sound effects and the making of *The Bridge on the River Wye*.
MARTIN: We had to edit out all the k's because of copyrights.
BONZAI: I was wondering if those comedic records and bizarre sounds had an effect on the songs you are better known for today. The production values of your work with the Beatles were certainly very unusual for pop records. Did those early comedy sessions influence your later work?
MARTIN: It was bound to, I suppose. You do what you do in the way which you think is right. So you build up a technique over the years, and I suppose a lot of that rubbed off in things like *Sgt. Pepper* and *Yellow Submarine*.
BONZAI: Let's find out about this shy guy who sits beside you, John Bur-

GEORGE MARTIN (LEFT) AND JOHN
BURGESS

gess. John, when did you join EMI?

BURGESS: 1951.

BONZAI: Is that where you two met?

BURGESS: We didn't actually meet at the beginning, because I was down at the factory. In those days it wasn't really a record company as such — two or three offices. My first job was to send out records. We didn't actually start working together until 1958.

BONZAI: Why have the two of you worked together so long?

BURGESS: [Cockney accent] Because we love each other.

MARTIN: When I left EMI in 1965, I thought I might be leaving behind some young people who were pretty good. I felt it would be smart to take them with me. Ronny Richards and Peter Sullivan came and I asked John to join our merry band. The four of us set up what is now AIR Studios in London.

BURGESS: I remember George saying to me, "The reason we're all getting together is that I am getting older, and you guys will have all the success and keep me in the manner to which I am accustomed." As it happened, the Beatles turned out to keep everybody. We all had individual successes, but obviously the biggest money earner was the Beatles.

MARTIN: We put everything back into the company; that's how AIR Studios began.

BONZAI: How did you come up with the name?

MARTIN: AIR stands for Associated Independent Recording. We thought of "AIR" first and then figured out the words to fit it.

BURGESS: The studio opened in October, 1969.

BONZAI: What about Montserrat?

MARTIN: That didn't happen until ten years later.

BONZAI: What was the reasoning there?

MARTIN: Madness.

BURGESS: No reason at all.

MARTIN: [Laughs] No, there was a reason. I was working a great deal in the States at the time and using other people's studios. But I always felt much more comfortable in our own studios. You get used to a way of working. I thought it would be a good idea to have a studio over here.

BURGESS: George is always coming up with crazy ideas. Previous to Montserrat, we spent a year and a half—

MARTIN: Two years…

BURGESS: —wandering around the world trying to find a boat big enough to put a studio on. We went to Malta—

MARTIN: Iceland, Yugoslavia, Poland…

BURGESS: —trying to find a boat so that George's dream studio would come to fruition.

MARTIN: And we did find a marvelous boat; it would have been fantastic. It was 160 feet long, twin screw…

BURGESS: A Yugoslavian ferry boat. A very good bargain, actually.

MARTIN: I wish we would have done it. It would have been a marvelous oceangoing studio, but oil prices tripled in 1973 and it meant that the overhead of running a diesel-powered ship would increase enormously. I was persuaded to abandon the project, and we built AIR Montserrat.

BONZAI: How's it working out?

MARTIN: It's a wonderful place…

BONZAI: Only one room?

MARTIN: Yes, only one room, but that's what we wanted. Basically, the whole point of going there is to have the place to yourself. You don't have people running around.

On the other hand, we've found that in the London studios, people like meeting up with other artists while recording.

BURGESS: Paul McCartney enjoys playing on other people's sessions and getting feedback from other musicians.

BONZAI: Chris Stone mentioned to me that he feels that the English have led the technical side of the industry in America.

MARTIN: It didn't used to be like that. In the early '50s at Abbey Road, I was always frustrated by the primitive machines we had to work with. Coming to this country and working at Capitol Records, I found 3-track recording. In England we had mono or stereo. You also had limiters and compressors that we didn't even know about.

But it's been a see-saw. The American studios sometimes have been ahead of us, sometimes behind us. It's not a question of a good machine being made in England, in America or in Japan. You might find a new device being made anywhere and it immediately becomes available worldwide. The range now is breathtaking. Facilities are better and, if you've got the money, the equipment range is incredible. Now it becomes a question not of who can design the best equipment, but who can afford it. It's an economical dilemma—such wonderful tools, but not everybody can afford them. Of course, worldwide, studios are suffering. There are too many studios, and record companies don't like spending money on studios. There's all the hot air of making first-class, digitally pure sound, but they don't want to pay for it. They want to pay the same money they paid in 1960.

BURGESS: Taking inflation into consideration, they probably are paying the same.

MARTIN: And yet, technology now is so expensive.

BONZAI: In the past few years, a lot of fine low-end equipment has become affordable, and home studios have become popular. The artist can do much of the work at home and then go into the big studio for the final mix. How is that affecting the art as well as the business of recording?

MARTIN: It's true that the amateur can now make marvelous records.

BURGESS: It's not just the amateur, though. Big-name artists are building their own small rooms.

MARTIN: And they're not so small, some of them.

BURGESS: I agree. Some of them are buying top-grade equipment and installing it in their own rooms. They spend three or four months doing their basic tracks, which they will later bring to the high-tech studios to finish up. It's certainly affected the studios in London.

We're finding that some of these artists equip their rooms, build a home studio, and then rent out their studios to themselves so they can pay for their own equipment. They are suddenly hit by the fact that they paid an awful lot of money for their equipment and they can't afford to just use it on their own projects. They have to bring in other people.

BONZAI: This must hurt the traditional commercial facilities.

BURGESS: Without a doubt. Phil Collins has a superb studio and he doesn't actually let it out in the commercial market, but he does lend it to friends.

BONZAI: Do you have any predictions for the next five years?

MARTIN: I think that the strong will survive and the weak will fail, as simple as that. The business is gradually changing, and the top class studios will go on being successful. The hybrid studio, the halfway house between a small studio and a professional one, will have a hard time of it.

BURGESS: And they won't be able to afford to keep up with the technology that is happening now.

MARTIN: Another fact is that there is a tremendous growth now in programming studios, where people build up their own little workshops at home with synths and computers. They are able to make up demos themselves—something I do if I want to get an idea across. Then all they need to finish the record is a really good recording facility. They will come to a big studio with programs and initial tracks.

BONZAI: Do you have your own workshop at home?

MARTIN: I've got a DX7 and a couple of other things, a very modest setup at home, because I have a very good programming room at AIR.

BONZAI: What about MIDI?

MARTIN: Well, we've equipped our studios at AIR so you can hook up MIDI with any one room and any other one, and be linked to our programming room. A group can be working in our number one studio, and if the keyboard player needs to have a particular synth sound, he can go into the programming room and work on that, while the other folks are work-

"Today's equipment range is incredible. Now it becomes a question not of who can design the best machine, but who can afford it. It's an economical dilemma—such wonderful tools, but not everybody can afford them."
—George Martin

ing on another track. Once he has his sound, he can go back into number one studio and play a keyboard there, using the sound from the programming room, because it's all connected up through MIDI. It's a useful development that has increased the versatility of the studio.

BONZAI: MIDI, computers, portable technology—more tools in the hands of more artists. But what about the reliance on programming and software and computerized music? Are things getting better, or are we creating a cyborg music industry?

MARTIN: I think it's making music boring. You hear the same sounds over and over again. Maybe I'm old fashioned, but I think the sound of a natural instrument is the best. One of the dangers of all this technology and eternal synthesized sound and programming and mechanics is that it is making music a bit sterile. These are wonderful tools if you use them properly, but if you use them to the detriment of real sounds, you get down a cul-de-sac of boring repetitions.

BONZAI: Maybe we're just children in a period of change and adjustment.

MARTIN: There's a danger, though. The kids are growing up with this facility at their fingertips. They're getting brainwashed to a certain extent. They might like to have some real sounds and get an orchestra and not quite know how to use it. They'd end up making the orchestra sound like a synth. If you're scoring for an orchestra, it's not just translating what you do on a keyboard and putting it into an orchestra.

For example, using a keyboard, you tend to make sounds on a synthesizer because you've got five fingers on the hand and those five fingers put notes together within the reach of the hand. You get bunched chords on a synth—a typical synth sound. Put that on a string orchestra, put your notes together like that, and you get a near synth-sound, too. But that's not good string work.

BONZAI: When you started out producing, you had to chop classical music into chunks to fit on 78s. Then came the LP, and now we have the CD with even greater playing time. How is this going to affect the approach to recording?

MARTIN: It seems to me that there have been no creative problems since the long-play record was introduced. We haven't really been inhibited too much. The CD gives us a wider range creatively, but the long-play vinyl did that. Before then it was very inhibiting. John, you remember making pop records in the pre-vinyl days and you had to make them within a definite time.

BURGESS: Usually under two minutes. That was the target we aimed for. In fact, Adam Faith had a hit which was one minute and 34 seconds long. In those days they wanted very short songs. I don't think I ever made anything longer than two minutes during the first few years.

MARTIN: In classical recordings it was terribly frustrating—chopping up movements and so on. I couldn't believe that a chairman of the company I worked for actually went on record saying that the long playing record was a flash in the pan and would never mean anything. I thought, what an idiot.

BONZAI: Last night, John told me that there is one subject that you've talked about quite enough—the Beatles. But I explained that I had a personal memory I wanted to discuss with you. You were the first producer I ever met. Abbey Road was the first studio I saw. And my first session was the night Ringo was tuning in the BBC for a track on "I Am the Walrus."

MARTIN WITH THE BEATLES,
CIRCA 1965

Later on in Scotland, I was studying *King Lear* and realized the song has lines from Act IV of the play. I don't remember you well—we met, but I was so overwhelmed with the experience. That night, John seemed to be running the show.

MARTIN: I wonder if I was there. [Laughs]

BONZAI: Oh, you were there, but you seemed more like a father figure. Ringo was reading a comic book and tuning the radio and John had his hands on those big gear shift faders. The next year, 1968, I was invited back for "Revolution #9" and I don't remember seeing you. George was raiding the EMI tape vaults, John was with Yoko by this time, I learned about splicing, and there was a flurry of activity with huge tape loops running across the room. Was there a period where your participation as a producer changed?

MARTIN: Yes, the accent changed, but both occasions you mention were when John was experimenting. John liked playing around, but he was not a very good technician. He couldn't handle equipment all that well, but he was always trying to get new and different effects. Now, the *King Lear* thing you're talking about—we used some of that on the record.

BONZAI: Yes, tuned right in off the radio and mixed in.

MARTIN: "I Am the Walrus" was at the mixing stage when you were there. It had already been recorded with cellos and horns and so on. "Revolution #9" was a melange of sounds. John was moving the faders around during "Walrus" because someone had to do something at random. After the Beatles ended, John went on to do even wilder things. He didn't have the great toyshop at Abbey Road, but he used to bring me cassettes. "George, can we make a record out of this?" It would be Yoko screaming in a bag. That was the kind of thing you were seeing in those sessions. In fact, it was in its infancy there. I'm not surprised that you would think that he was running the show. But he wasn't really running the show. He was being allowed to indulge himself.

Those sessions had grown out of something before that. The very first really successful bit of that type of work was "Tomorrow Never Knows," which started not with John, but with Paul. Paul had a Grundig tape recorder, and he found that by removing the erase head and putting a loop of tape on, he could saturate the tape with eternal sound by putting it into record. He could do just one lick on guitar and it would go round and round until it saturated itself and he'd have a loop. He would bring in a loop and make some weird sounds. The other boys, John and Ringo and George, would go away and do the same thing and bring me these strange sounds. Then I had to try to make something out of it all.

We would assemble them on different machines all over the place, listen to them forwards, backwards, at different speeds, and select which ones we liked and then have them continually going. It was like a primitive synthesizer. You had a loop turning over and if you opened up a fader, you would hear it. That's when the mix became a performance. While mixing, whatever you brought up at the time would be there. We wouldn't know what point of the loop would appear. It was a random thing. So, "Tomorrow Never Knows" can never be remixed again, because all those things happened at that time in that particular way. It's one of the greatest things about that record. It is a page in history that happened there, and it can't happen again.

BONZAI: I like that.

MARTIN: So did John. [Laughs]

BONZAI: This brings to mind the CD reissue of the work.

MARTIN: With "Tomorrow Never Knows" all we could do was take that existing master and clean it up a bit.

BONZAI: Have you done any other enhancements?

MARTIN: We actually remixed *Help* because it wasn't very good originally, and *Rubber Soul*, as well. Most of the later ones were really quite well recorded, if I do say so myself, and just required a little bit of cleaning up for CD.

As for the earlier ones, there is still a controversy about mono versus stereo in the early records. We might well go back and make some stereo versions.

BONZAI: Getting back to those moments of spontaneity and fun in the studio—do you still—

MARTIN: We still have fun in the studio, sure.

BURGESS: Not as much.

MARTIN: No, not as much as we used to.

BURGESS: That's one of the reasons I gave up production. It stopped being fun, and the artists don't seem to enjoy themselves in the studio as much these days.

MARTIN: There's no fun in taking three days to get a snare drum sound, which some people do.

BURGESS: But there is a slight trend toward returning to the past. When Anne Dudley did the music for the Phil Collins film *Buster*, she actually went into the studio and recorded everything at one go. There's a slight trend of going back and—

MARTIN: Giving a performance.

BURGESS: We had two or three sessions recently where everything was put down in one fell swoop.

MARTIN: I produced an album with Andy Leek, a new guy who is brilliant. All the rhythm tracks were done live and, in some cases, with horns at the same time. You get a great feeling in the studio. We didn't put down the definitive vocal, but he was singing along with them. So, everybody felt that they were performing. It does make a difference.

BONZAI: What a revolutionary idea.

BURGESS: Let's destroy all the sophisticated equipment and just go back to mono again.

MARTIN: Musicians should play together, but it doesn't happen much these days. I remember a session with a guitar player and a drummer who had never met. I said, "Wait a minute, you guys must know each other—you were on the same album." "No, we've been on the same albums many times, but we never met before." I thought, how crazy can it get?

BURGESS: Another effect, from the studio point of view, is that engineers don't have any experience for recording live musicians. All they can do is set up the mics for an overdubbing situation. Gather together four or five musicians—or even worse, a string section—and you have to look hard for a capable engineer.

BONZAI: Is the role of producer changing?

MARTIN: The role of producer has already changed. There are more engineer/producers now. I'm the old-fashioned type, a producer who is a musician and likes to work with an engineer who's an engineer. I think that the two roles are very difficult to combine. I feel that the guy who concentrates on the art, the production and the music, shouldn't really be bothered with whether the microphone is on the blink or not, or whether the EQ switch is dirty or not.

Similarly, I think the engineer should be concentrating on his work and not have to deal with the tantrums of a drummer who is feeling a pain in his back. There are distinct problems, but if you have these guys working in harmony, it's the best possible team you can get. Having said that, the majority of producers now are in fact engineer/producers. Some of them do it extraordinarily well.

As for the future, people are tending to do more things themselves. I'm afraid that maybe I've had something to do with that, but I think the role of producer has become a bit too important. Because of that, people say "I want to produce. I want to do this myself. Look at my album—I produced it myself!" It's a boast, and I don't think it should be. I think they should say, "Let's get a good producer to help us." The star is still the writer, and the singer is still the most important part of a record.

▼ ▼ ▼

EDDY OFFORD
Yes Man

"*You must stop copying other bands.*"

I F YOU PULL out a few of your vintage Yes albums, you'll notice the credits read, "Produced by Yes and Eddy Offord." Starting out as a musician in the late '60s, Offord quickly switched to engineering and then assumed the new and coveted role of engineer/producer.

Offord was at the center of the seminal English sound of the early '70s, producing and engineering seven monsters for Yes and a couple for Emerson, Lake and Palmer. He engineered Pink Floyd for Antonioni's *Zabriskie Point* and worked on *The Last Waltz* and Showtime's *Synchronicity World Tour* for The Police. Other notable credits include several tracks on John Lennon's *Imagine*, riding herd on the R.C.O. Allstars (featuring Dr. John, Booker T., Levon Helm, Steve Cropper and Donald "Duck" Dunn), as well as respectable projects with Todd Rundgren, Thin Lizzy and the Dregs.

Ah, Yes. The band began its classic rock odyssey in 1968, progressing through various line-ups, including distinctive vocalist Jon Anderson, keyboardists Rick Wakeman and Tony Kaye, drummers Bill Bruford and Alan White, guitarist Steve Howe and bassist Chris Squire.

When I think of Yes, I hear the angelic choruses balanced with the dark rumblings of British power rock. The music cranks up a mighty machine and then drops down to Earth with delicate acoustic passages and baroque synth excursions. You're allowed to catch your breath, leaving space in the drama. The rhythm and dynamics slap you around, creating an operatic, quick-cut cinematic effect. Let's meet the man behind the experience: Eddy Offord.

▼▼▼

BONZAI: You're most associated with Yes...
OFFORD: Along with Emerson, Lake and Palmer, I would say so.
BONZAI: Do you like that identification?
OFFORD: Yes, because that kind of music was very acclaimed for its sound: the clarity. That music really lends itself to exploration for an engineer.
BONZAI: When you refer to that clarity of sound, what years are you thinking of?
OFFORD: The early '70s, 24-track and sometimes even 16-track recording. I've seen the whole recording scene change in the time I've been involved.
BONZAI: Let's go back to your formative years. You were a musician first, a guitar player.
OFFORD: I used to play in a band, starting out in the English equivalent of

▼▼▼
BY MR. BONZAI

high school. I always loved music. And just by coincidence I was looking for a holiday job and saw an ad for a sound engineer trainee. I thought I'd give it a shot, and when I got in the studio and saw the musicians playing, and those big speakers, I was sold.

At night I'd finish a session and have my band waiting around the corner. We'd pretend like we were closing up the studio, and then I'd play guitar, record and mix in the off time.

BONZAI: I've been listening again to some of those early recordings, and what strikes me is the wham-bam, hard left, hard right, sweep-across-the-speakers stereo. I miss some of those wild things we used to hear, like footsteps going from one side of the room to the other, lead vocals hard right and chorus hard left: a cinematic feeling to the sound.

OFFORD: Obviously, since I first started there have been many developments in the way in which things are recorded. Unfortunately, I think it has become a bit too homogenized. Every sound is so huge that you can hardly tell one band from another. Guitars tend to be multilayered, and the drums might be live, but they have samples added. Everything sounds bigger than life. This is cool, but I think there is a tendency to lose the identity of the band behind that wash of sound, if you know what I mean.

BONZAI: Exactly. In listening to your work, there is an impression of an immense sound, but when you start analyzing it, there are relatively few elements involved.

OFFORD: Yes, you can actually tell what each member of the band is playing.

BONZAI: In the Yes recordings, there is dramatic buildup and then suddenly the bottom will drop out and you showcase one lone acoustic instrument. A lot of dynamics and space. Were you responsible for that?

OFFORD: Yes.

BONZAI: I mentioned to a seasoned engineer, Bill Dooley, that I was going to be meeting you, and he said, "He's my idol! He's the reason I got into this business."

OFFORD: Oh dear.

BONZAI: He felt that you were one of the first engineers to get credit where credit was due. Is that true? Are you one of the guys who elevated the position of the engineer?

OFFORD: I would say so, yes. Way back when I started, the engineer was more of a technician and didn't really contribute that much artistically. He was just told to do things. I think Glyn Johns and myself were among the first crop of engineers who turned into producers.

BONZAI: Did you push for it, or was it the chemistry of the situations?

Eddy
Offord

OFFORD: It was the chemistry. I had engineered one album with Yes, called *Time and a Word*, which didn't do very well at all. Then Phil Carson from Atlantic said that the band didn't really need a producer. I was asked to co-produce with them. The very first album that we did together was a big hit, *The Yes Album*.

BONZAI: How did that relationship fit with the band members?

OFFORD: Basically, there were a lot of different factions in Yes, and they had contrary tastes and feelings about the music. I would try to channel all this high energy of wanting to do everything and act as a mediator, a referee, trying to figure out what ideas were good and which were bad.

BONZAI: Were there ever any arguments?

OFFORD: Yes. [Laughs] And I was the one who was called on to make the peace.

BONZAI: Let's talk about ego—for the artist, the engineer, the producer.

OFFORD: Purely as an engineer, you must have very little ego, because you are dealing with big enough egos as it is and another one just doesn't help. As an engineer/producer, you have to be a little more forceful and stand up for what you think. But I've always been flexible. I've gone by the philosophy that if someone has an idea, it takes just as long to argue about it as it takes to try it. If you try the idea, the speakers don't lie. Either it works or it doesn't.

In the band, 90 percent of the ideas were terrible, but there were that 10 percent that were really great. If you rejected every idea from a particular member, you could lose out on something that might really work. I kept an open mind about other people's suggestions.

BONZAI: So there was a certain amount of experimentation going on?

OFFORD: Yes, we did all sorts of wild things.

BONZAI: Did you keep the outtakes?

OFFORD: Not really. With Yes it was a very different process. Some of the songs were 20 minutes long. They never played the song from top to bottom. We'd do the first musical section, which might be 30 seconds long, and work on it until they were happy with it. We'd do it section by section, so there were no outtakes. The 24-track was a series of splices.

BONZAI: Didn't that cause trouble in re-creating it on stage?

OFFORD: No, not at all. Once the album was finished, the band would have to learn how to play it. [Laughs] At some point after the *Fragile* album, they talked me into coming on the road with them and doing live sound and making them sound like they did on record—even better, hopefully. I had two tape machines so that I could just cue in—although it wasn't a Milli Vanilli-type thing—certain overdubs that they couldn't accomplish all at the same time. Maybe a church organ here or a vocal part there to add a touch of the record.

BONZAI: This was in the period of the *Yessongs* live triple album?

OFFORD: Yes, and I was on the road with them for four or five years. It changed my life totally. I was just this young kid who had grown up in a recording studio. All I'd seen in my life were those four walls, and suddenly I was touring America, Japan, Europe, Australia. Doing a lot of partying, meeting girls. One thing it did teach me was that when you go out on the road with a band, when you do the same show every night, most times it's good, a few times it's terrible and a few times it's really magical. You can't forecast it. On those magical evenings, you come off feeling so uplifted.

BONZAI: Does "Roundabout" have a backward tape at the beginning?

OFFORD: Yes, a backward piano. It took quite a long time to assemble it, because it meant picking the right notes and editing it all together.

BONZAI: When you take it apart, it's a pretty strange combination: an acoustic guitar with a backward tape, a technical maneuver. One of the most distinctive instrumental hooks in popular music.

OFFORD: Well, in some ways, people were a little more daring, more creative back then. I love the bigness of the sounds today, but like anything else, it gets overdone. After the flange was invented, you heard flanging on every record. I guess the first ones were Small Faces on "Itchycoo Park." They did a very tasteful thing, but then, of course, it was all overdone and everyone phased everything up the wazoo. Every new recording technique that comes out usually starts very tastefully and then gets overdone. I would like to see the new technology right alongside some of the earlier technologies, so that you get the feeling of hearing a band. I'd like places in the song without huge drum sounds—clean and clear, so you can hear what the drummer's inflections are. And maybe in other parts of the song you can go for the wall of sound. But to have that wall there all the time gets extremely boring.

BONZAI: In that era of Yes; Emerson, Lake and Palmer; Pink Floyd; Moody Blues; and Genesis, there was a very powerful thing happening in England. I imagine that there was a healthy competitiveness, of trying to top one another, which resulted in all these seminal records. What's your take on that time?

OFFORD: I think we took more chances back then. We really got 110 percent out of the equipment, which was pretty meager. We were forced to be innovative. Yes, there was competition. Especially for me, working with Emerson, Lake and Palmer and Yes at the same time. They were jealous of one another when I was working with one or the other. They all had their own individual sounds, but they were competing to a certain extent.

In general, my success comes down to my ability to get along with people and make them feel good and create the right atmosphere, more than it is my engineering expertise. That's the most important quality that someone in my position can have.

BONZAI: Right now you're doing a boxed set, a Yes collection?

OFFORD: You know, it's a funny situation. I worked with a band a few years back called Platinum Blonde and they went five times platinum. Some albums go straight up the charts and then straight down. You never hear from them again.

With Yes, I keep hearing this bloody music on the radio. It does sound a

> "**I** *think we took more chances back then. We really got 110 percent out of the equipment, which was pretty meager. We were forced to be innovative.*"

bit dated to me nowadays. On this boxed set, I'm actually going in and remixing a few tracks, like "Close to the Edge." I don't want to lose the integrity of what was happening back then, but I know that with the modern devices around today, I can make it sound even better.

BONZAI: So you're not going to offend the religious fans?

OFFORD: I'm going to be extremely careful not to! [Laughs] No, I'm not going to put drum machines all over it. I just want to do it tastefully, but better.

BONZAI: That was an interesting period. Do you think audiences today are as profoundly moved? Back then the music was a lifestyle. You locked onto bands then.

OFFORD: I think the younger generation have their heroes as much as we had back then. And I also think that things are starting to change a bit in the music business. Bands like R.E.M. don't go for this heavy production stuff. They just want to do their thing. I think there is a cycle, and as each generation comes up they go through what we did. I have a 20-year-old stepdaughter, and she cries when she sees some bands. She went to see a U2 concert, and she was crying all the way through it. It was so emotional. So, I guess it's the same for them, too.

BONZAI: Let's touch on some of the other people you've worked with. Tell me about the *Synchronicity* world tour.

OFFORD: We did live recording. I went out on the road with The Police and studied all the musical cues for four or five dates, made notes, and when I was together on it we brought in a huge truck and recorded for two or three weeks. Then we went into the studio and fixed a few bum notes here and there, and Sting resang some vocal parts. We had women singers on that tour, and we double-tracked them back in the studio. I think it came off very well.

BONZAI: John Lennon?

OFFORD: I recorded "Jealous Guy" and "I Don't Want to Be a Soldier Mama" for the *Imagine* album. What happened is that I started the album out and it was going really well. It was a very magical experience for me, but I was so into the progressive rock thing at the time that I told John and Yoko that I couldn't continue on with the album because I had prior commitments. I started the album and then had to withdraw from the project.

BONZAI: What was it like?

OFFORD: It was really great. He had a sixth sense and an awareness about him that you could feel. Although he hadn't gone to great schools or studied and wasn't extremely sophisticated in terms of some things, he had this soul that just shone through everything. Yoko was the intelligent one in the family: a smart lady, and a nice lady. I liked her, although I hated it when she sang.

BONZAI: You've worked with a few other people whom I greatly admire. What about Dr. John?

OFFORD: Oh, yeah, it was great working with him. It was up in Woodstock, N.Y. I had my own studio there for about 15 years, a unique place in the sense that I set up in the same room with the musicians. And Levon Helm had this huge barn and house, which we used. Levon played drums. Steve Cropper on guitar, "Duck" Dunn on bass, the *Saturday Night Live* horn section. It was a great assembling of musicians and a lot of fun. The hardest part was getting them all to be in the same room at the same time to play. Before we started recording, Dr. John actually did an hour's

> "There were a lot of different factions in Yes, and they had contrary tastes and feelings about the music. I would try and channel all this high energy and act as a mediator, a referee, trying to figure out what ideas were good and which were bad."

ritual where he went around the outside with incense and blessed the studio.

BONZAI: I bet it helped.

OFFORD: [Laughs] I think it did, yeah.

BONZAI: No doubt you're fairly wrapped up in today's technology. Have you got any new tricks up your sleeve?

OFFORD: There is a whole array of toys out there. So many signal processors, which I think people tend to overuse. I would like to mention the speakers that I'm using, though — Radian.

BONZAI: These are close-field monitors?

OFFORD: Yes, but while using them I've heard comments like "Let's hear what it sounds like on the little speakers." And I say, "Well, those are the little speakers." I think they give you a tendency to put a little bit more middle and high-end than you would with the Yamahas, which are sort of the industry standard.

I'm also using a processing thing called Spherical Sound. There are other systems that are similar, like QSound, which Madonna used. Roland is supposed to be bringing one out. This one is quite sophisticated. It's a nice addition as a processing thing, to space a sound out.

BONZAI: Of all the people you've worked with, who is the most outstanding, the most amazing artist, the genius?

OFFORD: There have been a few, but David Sancious is one for sure. He's not very well known, but he's an incredible keyboard player: one of the best ever. He toured with Sting, and he's played with Peter Gabriel. I did two solo albums with him. They weren't phenomenal commercial successes, but a lot of musicians enjoyed the albums.

BONZAI: Any advice for those aspiring to your position? Is there any shortcut?

OFFORD: You must stop copying other bands. I have this theory: England is about the size of one of your states here in America, but so much innovative music has come out of England. The reason is partly the lousy weather, that the pubs close at 11, and that the TV and radio are totally screwed up. You can't just switch on the radio and get whatever you like. They play a little bit of this and a little bit of that, and it drives you around the bend. So, bands go into their garages and come up with things that are new.

American bands are so exposed to radio and MTV that they try too much to copy. Obviously, you have to draw from your influences, but there is a fine line between that and sheer copying. You have to believe in what you are doing, and you have to have your own sound and approach to music. Draw influences, but don't emulate.

I also think that the music business has changed a lot. Earlier on, people were more daring and adventurous. Today, if Yes was a new band and they came along to the record company with 15- and 20-minute songs, they'd say, "Get outta here!" The record companies are responsible for saying to an artist, "Listen to Madonna, Michael Jackson — that's what you should be doing." They are also culpable.

▼▼▼

HUGH PADGHAM
Studio
Synchronicity

▼▼▼

BY MR. BONZAI

Hugh Padgham is at the peak of his career as producer/mixer/ engineer. He's produced and recorded artists such as Phil Collins, Sting, The Police, David Bowie and Paul McCartney, engineered and/or mixed Genesis, Peter Gabriel, Brian Wilson, Suzanne Vega, Hall & Oates and Julia Fordham, and has numerous awards on his mantel, including 1985 Grammys for Producer and Album of the Year. Just goes to show what can happen when you get your ears, your mind and your hands in synchronicity.

▼▼▼

BONZAI: You and Sting go way back, don't you?
PADGHAM: We certainly do. I first worked with Sting on a project unrelated to The Police when I was an engineer at Virgin Studios in London. He was doing a production project soon after the beginning of The Police, and I was the designated engineer at The Townhouse. That's where we originally met.
BONZAI: How did you make the move from engineer to engineer/producer?
PADGHAM: Mainly by accident. When I started at The Townhouse in 1978, I was engineer there, and one day a session came in. The producer happened to be a guy named Steve Lillywhite, and we hit it off from the word go. He ended up doing all of his work at The Townhouse because it was the hip place to work in those days. Through Steve, we ended up doing lots of work, including two XTC albums together and an album with Peter Gabriel. That is how I met Phil Collins; we did songs like "The Intruder" and "No Self Control" on Peter Gabriel's third album. When we finished the album three or four months later, Phil's manager rang me up and told me that Phil was interested in doing a solo album and asked if I would like to produce it with him. With the success of that album, I got asked to do other productions. And also through my work with XTC; they were on tour with The Police, who were looking for another producer. Andy Partridge from XTC recommended me. Since Sting had worked with me before, he said they'd give me a try. All a bunch of lucky accidents, but I think that's how everyone's career gets off the ground.
BONZAI: The Police were really a breakthrough—a simple trio translated

so well musically, so powerfully. In your mind, why did it have such a big impact?

PADGHAM: Well, I don't think while you're in the studio you ever realize that you are doing something that might end up to be so special. I was just trying to relate the music to the recording medium. I think it was partly because I was the new boy on the scene, and Sting was writing songs that were somewhat more serious in terms of music and lyrics. I was able to understand what Sting was doing musically, and it all worked out well. I didn't do anything special or different for me at all. It was just me in the studio with them, and it gelled.

BONZAI: Is it difficult for you to travel from country to country, studio to studio?

PADGHAM: No, not really. Nowadays it's much easier than it used to be, because most studios have similar equipment. When I first started as a freelance engineer, there weren't that many freelancers around and you would go to studios that had very particular equipment. Now, most studios have either an SSL or a Neve console, and you just get to know how they work. After a few days you understand the anomalies of the studio. To me, it's no problem at all, apart from being away from home.

BONZAI: What are the basic pieces of equipment that you rely on as you travel around?

PADGHAM: My main source of reference are my own monitor speakers. I use these Acoustic Research AR-18Ls. They're similar in size to Yamaha NS-10s, but they sound quite different. I've used them for ten years now and they haven't even made them for five years. When I heard that they

PADGHAM IN THE STUDIO WITH STING

stopped making the AR-18Ls, I bought all the existing ones from the factory—about ten pairs. The first or second album I ever mixed on these was *H₂0* for Hall & Oates. I went to Bob Ludwig at Master Disk in New York, and I was a little worried because I had mixed it on these little speakers that only cost 100 pounds because the main monitors were no good. And he told me he couldn't believe the sound of this record. We did virtually no EQ'ing to transfer the tape to the disk. This was before the days of CD. He gave me major confidence in the mixes I thought sounded good. Ever since then, I've used these speakers.

BONZAI: Shall we touch on consoles? What's your comfortable mode of desk these days?

PADGHAM: I like to mix on SSL because it's a bit like driving a car. You don't think about it, rather like steering around a corner or changing gears. I know the console so well that I can more or less operate it with my eyes closed. Being able to work on a console where I don't have to think technically is very important. And I've been involved with SSL from the early days, because we had one of the first production consoles in Studio 2 at The Townhouse.

BONZAI: Tape machines?

PADGHAM: I hoped that you wouldn't get around to that question.

BONZAI: Let me put it this way: On the new Phil Collins album, I noticed it said drums and bass were recorded on analog.

PADGHAM: This is my big problem with digital: I think good digital recorders, such as the 3348 or the 3324 with Apogee filters, do sound faithful, but I don't love the sound of drums and bass off digital. I like what analog tape does to the sound, as far as making a record is concerned.

BONZAI: When you do the final mix, are you running an analog multi-track alongside a digital and combining the two?

PADGHAM: In the case of Phil's album, yes. Just synched up with a Lynx. The digital machine is absolutely fantastic, because you are able to bounce without generation loss. I do a lot of recording for such things as vocals with four takes and then combine to one track. On analog you are losing a generation when you combine, but with digital you're not. The other great thing with digital is that you can choose your crossfade times and your splice angle, which isn't possible on an analog machine when you're dropping in. You can get away with murder doing drop-ins and drop-outs on a digital machine.

BONZAI: Let's talk about two vocalists you work with, Sting and Phil. What is the difference in approach to getting their voices on tape?

PADGHAM: With Phil, we have a setup we've used for some time, and Phil feels quite comfortable with it. He actually sings to the sound of his voice going through this setup, which is basically a cheap mic and a cheap compressor.

BONZAI: Can you reveal the actual tools?

PADGHAM: I will, because what sounds good on Phil doesn't necessarily sound good on other people. I've tried this particular setup on Sting, and it doesn't sound good. On Phil I use a Beyer M88, a dynamic mic (which he also uses onstage). It gives a nice rough edge to his voice, and then we go through an Allen & Heath minilimiter. It's a vicious limiter, but it's fantastic for me because it works well with Phil. I can set my VU meter with this limiter, and it's like the meter hits a brick wall, wherever you set it: 0 or +1, or whatever. With Phil I know I've got his sound, and I don't have to look at the console again when I'm doing his vocals. I can concentrate on what and how he's singing. This limiter has a slow attack and a fast release. It gives that guttural sound to his voice.

BONZAI: How about getting Sting on tape?

PADGHAM: Well, Sting is an experienced singer. He's got good microphone technique, and I'm still looking for the perfect mic. I've used all sorts: an 87, an AKG 414. We've been doing a lot of vocals in the control room for this new album, and I've been using a Sennheiser 441, mainly because it has a tight cardioid response for when we use the big speakers in the control room. I'm not getting too much leakage on the mic and, of course, my level can be that much higher before it feeds back.

BONZAI: When you're working on a project, recording and mixing, do you visualize the music?

PADGHAM: It's not that I think of it in visual terms; I get a concept when I hear a song. Almost immediately, I have a feeling of where I am going to put delays or reverb. I get a vibe and keep fiddling around until it equals what I'm thinking in my head.

BONZAI: I've been studying Phil Collins' *But Seriously*, and it's very complex. There's a lot of material there. How do you keep everything clear? How do you keep it from getting muddy?

PADGHAM: When we're putting parts down in the studio, I have a quick realization whether the parts are going to work against each other musically and from an audio point of view. When I produce or mix a record, I hear the music in a sort of sonic spectrum. Obviously, if you have too many things in the same register, they are going to work against each other from a sonic point of view. I work hard on musical arrangements when I'm producing with the artist so that there are few things in the same sonic spectral area. I make a big sound out of as few elements as possible. When Phil and I are working together in the studio, we say, "Okay, we'll have a bass player in this evening. We'll have a guitar player in this week." When we do Phil Collins' records, they're completely overdubbed. Whereas, when I'm working with Sting, there is a band in the studio.

BONZAI: Do you have a preference?

PADGHAM: No, because they are both interesting.

BONZAI: Are there any of your peers you especially admire?

PADGHAM: The list is probably endless, although as a peer, Bob Clearmountain deserves a special mention. I'm lucky enough to work with some incredible people in the music business. I'm probably the luckiest person in the world, to be able to work with Sting. I respect him as a musician and as a person I like to work with in the studio.

BONZAI: Are there any exceptional artists you've worked with and felt they were overlooked?

PADGHAM: Yes, I think a lot of projects are like that, because not everything you do becomes a hit. I'm very proud to work with Phil Collins, Sting and Peter Gabriel. I couldn't choose better people to work with, but I think that groups like XTC deserve greater recognition.

BONZAI: How about Split Enz?

PADGHAM: Exactly what I was going to say next. Split Enz, to me, were one of the best bands ever and I did two records for them. They were bril-

"Pop music is very transient. Van Gogh and Monet were not particularly respected in their own lifetimes, but luckily for us the medium is still there to look at and appreciate a hundred years later. Pop music is dispensable."

liant and it's a huge shame that they never made it in a bigger way. My problem with pop music is the lowest common denominator factor; unfortunately, what I think is good doesn't necessarily appeal to Martha in St. Louis.

BONZAI: Yes, it's a crying shame that a very good record may fail because of timing or promotion. If it doesn't make it during its release time, it disappears and has no chance of being rediscovered.

PADGHAM: Pop music is very transient. Van Gogh and Monet were not particularly respected in their own lifetimes, but luckily for us, the medium is still there to look at and appreciate a hundred years later. Pop music is dispensable. That's why I prefer to work with people like Sting, who are making albums for the sake of music, not just for making a hit record. I know he has some hit records, but I enjoy making music I will be proud of for years to come.

BONZAI: How old are you?

PADGHAM: 35.

BONZAI: Ah, just a lad.

PADGHAM: Yes, a lad, no less. Everyone in America always thinks I'm about 50. When I meet new people in the studio, they go, "You're so young!" It's weird for me, because I was a struggling tape-op and assistant engineer for years.

BONZAI: Any advice for survival in this studio game?

PADGHAM: When you're not in the studio, it's a good idea to do something else. I have interests outside of music, and one of them is trying to keep healthy, because the studio is not a very healthy environment. I try to keep as fit as possible. The other bent I have is motor racing. I'm a complete motor racing fanatic, and I have a part ownership in a prominent English racing car team, Richard Lloyd Racing.

BONZAI: Would you consider yourself a good businessman?

PADGHAM: No, that's why I have a manager. Dennis Muirhead has guided me since just before I did Phil Collins' first solo album. And I've involved him in the motor racing team as well.

BONZAI: Do you have any business tips for those who are entering a competitive industry?

PADGHAM: I say I am not a businessman, but I have strong ideas for business. One rather obvious thing I haven't gone into as a business venture is owning my own recording studio. Number one, I've had the honor to be involved in the Fisher Lane Farm studios, the Genesis studio in Surrey, England. That's where we did the last Genesis album and Phil's last album. It's a fantastic studio, and we built the control room about five years ago from the ground up. It's the best control room that we could build. I'm proud to have been involved, but basically I haven't gone for my own studio because when I work with artists, it's important to work in the environment they want to be in. When AIR Montserrat existed, Sting loved the studio and wanted to do his records there. If I had a studio in London, we would be at loggerheads and my studio would be empty in London. I would also get bored working in my own studio all the time. I find it a challenge to work in other studios, with different acoustic environments, different equipment. It keeps me on my toes as an engineer. And I still enjoy engineering.

BONZAI: Can you see yourself as just a producer, forgoing the engineering side of things?

"I get a concept when I hear a song. Almost immediately, I have a feeling of where I am going to put delays or reverb. I get a vibe and keep fiddling around until it equals what I'm thinking in my head."

PADGHAM: No, not really. I've tried it once or twice, and I always end up sort of knocking the engineer out of the way and fiddling with the knobs, because I know exactly what I want to hear. It seems stupid to try to relay it through someone else, when all it takes is twiddling a few knobs to get what I want without explaining it to anyone else.

BONZAI: Have you ever had any particularly ridiculous experiences in the studio?

PADGHAM: Oh, yes, but I'm sure they're too censorable. I think craziness in the studio happens less now because the music business is much more on a budget. It's more serious now, but when I first started, at a studio called Advision in London [now closed], it was different. I'd only been there three or four weeks, and I was on a session with Mott the Hoople. One night, everyone was very drunk, and they wanted a crash or explosion to follow a sax line. We just couldn't get a sound that was good enough. One of the guys saw this metal tea tray, which I used for bringing tea. He took it and whacked it on his knee and thought it sounded great. So we went out into the studio and one of the band members kneeled on the floor while another smashed it on his head. I had to mike his head up!

BONZAI: How many takes?

PADGHAM: There were enough takes that the tea tray became so mangled he couldn't hit him over the head any more. The bass player, Overend Watts, was doing the hitting. The other guy was lying on the floor with an 87 about two feet away, going "Harder, hit me harder!"

PADGHAM AND SHERYL CROW AT BROOKLYN RECORDING STUDIO

BONZAI: Andy Summers told me about people getting covered with trash if they fell asleep in the studio.

PADGHAM: That's right—in Montserrat, we had this couch in front of the desk, which was the kiss of death because it was so comfortable. We were so active, swimming and running during the days, that during the evening anybody who sat on the couch immediately fell asleep. We would then cover the person with as much stuff as we could find, bits of tape and such, as well as painting him and whatever else you could do. Eventually, the person would wake up with all this stuff crashing off around him. On the best of occasions, we would just leave the person, who would wake up at three in the morning all alone and well decorated. We called it "sending someone to the party."

BONZAI: Are you still having fun in the studio?

PADGHAM: Oh, absolutely. Going into the studio with a band is like a breath of fresh air. We go in and have a good time, but also there are serious undercurrents. Having a good time reflects in the music, and it's so difficult to capture that feeling on records sometimes.

▼▼▼

JOHN POTOKER
Doing What Feels Right

"*The best thing is to
create a marriage
between the technology
and people.*"

▼▼▼

BY NICK VALLELONGA

THE HEADLINE IN the April 16, 1988, *Billboard* read: "Potoker and Jones Give New Order Tune New Life." "Potoker" refers to producer/engineer John Potoker, and "Jones" is Quincy Jones. Any time your name gets mentioned in front of Quincy Jones' in an article about music, you must be doing something right. Potoker's production and remix credits include Herb Alpert, the Four Tops, Phil Collins, Genesis, Go 101, Toni Childs, New Order, the Pointer Sisters and Quincy Jones. It's an impressive list, and the diversity reflects Potoker's background in varied types of music.

His father was John Potoker Sr., who in the 1940s was considered one of the top pianists in the country, playing primarily with the Tommy Dorsey Band and then with Benny Goodman. After the big band era ended, Potoker Sr. became an accomplished studio musician, working with various artists and on jingles. It was here that the seeds for John Jr.'s musical influences were planted: He learned music theory from old jazz masters, and he also became interested in recording.

As a teen he played with local bands, but he tired of that grind and started working as a DJ in clubs and on the radio. Eventually, though, he decided his calling was in the recording studio, and he managed to land a succession of dues-paying jobs at small studios and jingle houses. His big break came when he got a job as an engineer at Sigma Sound in NYC. His engineering credits from this period are extensive, including Madonna and Ashford & Simpson.

Mix caught up with Potoker at his home recording studio in New Jersey, in a townhouse looking out on the Manhattan skyline.

▼▼▼

MIX: When did you first feel that you had really contributed to the sound of a track or an album?
POTOKER: That was with the Talking Heads and Brian Eno on *Remain in Light*. I felt very comfortable in that I was allowed to contribute a lot to what was going down. In fact, at times it felt like I could move from engineering and pick up an instrument and start playing it. Eno was generous in allowing me to start things on my own. He liked to feed off situations, and he was really into sound treatments. The things that we developed on

those records were all started from him, but he allowed other people their creative input.

MIX: That must have been a great experimental period for you.

POTOKER: Yeah, we did some wild things. I remember a track on another record with Eno and David Byrne, *My Life in the Bush of Ghosts*, where we lifted a vocal track off another record. The interesting thing was that before sampling and all this controversy about lifting things from records, we were doing that—I guess it was '79 or '80. We were lifting things off cassettes, off the radio, wherever we could get them. We would put them on 1/4-inch tape and then fly them into different sections of the multitrack and actually make a tune out of them. We ended up patching out of this one vocal into a key that's used to send SOS messages. And that would trigger the sound. So the vocal could be played with rhythmically; you could tap out a beat on this thing, and the vocal would open on and off, which was very effective.

MIX: To what do you attribute your growth as an artist?

POTOKER: Initially you just pick things up along the way. You've got to experiment with engineering techniques and let your ears be the judge. As far as production techniques, I've been fortunate to work alongside some great producers, and I was able to see the differences in the way they work and pick out the good things about each person.

MIX: You have worked with some great producers and artists. Let me throw out some names to you. Phil Ramone.

POTOKER: Yeah, Phil's great. I've actually never recorded for Phil; I've just done some mixing for him. It's a situation where he basically lets me go and do my thing. We may be working in the same studio, and he may be in

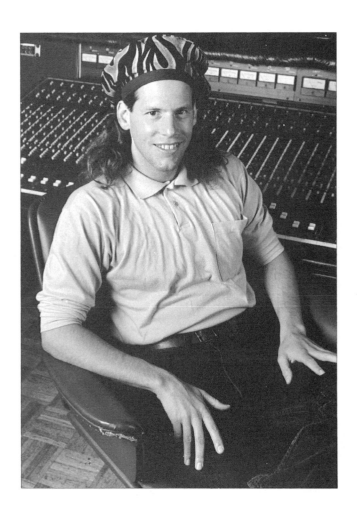

a session upstairs while I'm working downstairs, so he'll come in with fresh ears and listen. Actually, Phil is a lot like my high school football coach in that he presents you with a situation and tries to psych you up for the job that's ahead of you and tries to get you to do your best.

MIX: Quincy Jones.

POTOKER: Quincy was supervising a remix and post-production that I was doing for a New Order tune ["Blue Monday"] on his label, Qwest. Quincy's "The Master." He reminds me of Yoda from *Star Wars*. Quincy will go through the tracks with me and pick things out he likes and bounce them off me to see if I can get into where his head is at. I find it incredibly stimulating to work with people of that caliber.

MIX: Phil Collins released a CD called *Phil Collins 12-inchers*, where five of the six tracks were remixes that you produced. That's quite a compliment. How did you start working with Phil?

POTOKER: I was at The Townhouse in London working on some other things. Phil had just come in to start a record. I was working with Steve Chase, who used to assist on all of Phil's projects. Phil had just finished up some work with Philip Bailey and was working on his own record, and on the weekends he was working on the Band Aid Christmas record. He had to do the 12-inch on the Philip Bailey project, and Steve recommended me. So I have Steve to thank for connecting me with Phil.

Phil told me that he had this song called "Easy Lover," and he asked if I was interested in doing [the 12-inch]. He needed it right away, and I had to get it done by the end of the weekend. So while Phil was doing his thing for the Christmas record, I was in the other studio mixing.

It was one of those things where I really got off on what I was doing, and I ended up staying in the studio for two days. About 10 o'clock Monday morning, Phil came in fresh, had a little breakfast, and I had the song ready for playback. Phil, Hugh Padgham and Phil's guitar player Daryl Strummer were there. I *knew* during the playback that I had nailed the tune, and Phil waited till Daryl and Hugh left the room and he said, "You know, if I had thought of that intro, I would have used it on my version." Since then, I've done most of his remixes and some Genesis things.

MIX: We've talked about some producers you've worked with. Now let's talk about you as a producer. You were recently working in Australia.

POTOKER: I went to Australia to produce a band called Go 101. They're from Melbourne, and it's a new band, so there were a lot of problems you encounter working with a new band—getting them used to recording in the studio, etc.

MIX: Are there certain types of equipment you specifically request to have in a studio?

POTOKER: Not really. But the studio has to be maintained. When I walk into a studio, I expect whatever I see in front of me to work.

MIX: Do you prefer digital recording or analog?

POTOKER: I guess a combination of both is the way to go, if you're fortunate enough to have the budget. The good thing about digital is that it's quiet: You don't get tape hiss, and the signal is not going to change from repetitive playback. With analog tape, running the same material over the heads changes it throughout the course of a project. There are ways to work around it, but why go through the hassle if you don't have to?

MIX: You are primarily known for your mixing and your 12-inch production. Where would you like to go next?

POTOKER: I'm into working on quality projects, no matter what capacity. I mixed an album for A&M for Toni Childs, which was a great record to get involved with. When I heard the rough on the cassette, the songs and music were really different from what people know me to do. And then I found out that David Rickets from the band David & David had co-written some of the stuff, and co-produced, and he was someone I wanted to work with. It was a new opportunity, a new artist and a nice album to work on.

MIX: What attracts you to producing a new artist?

POTOKER: It's got to be someone who's really confident. First, they've got to have the songs. I respond to the songs. If the songs are there, then I'll pursue it and find out more about the artist or the band.

MIX: How do you feel about the technology affecting today's music?

POTOKER: For a while, I was a member of a very techno-oriented band, Doppelganger. But even in the context of that band, you had excellent musicianship. There's so much to be said for live feel, and the best thing is to create a marriage between the technology and people. I don't think manufactured music is going to fool anybody. There's got to be a feeling to the music. The disadvantage of technology is that there are so many different keyboards, samplers and libraries of sounds to choose from that perhaps people are not that anxious or curious about going out and miking their own things. Whenever I use a sample on a record, it's a sample that I created, that I went out and miked, that I compressed or did whatever I needed to do to get the sound. That's my personal stamp, and I want to continue it. I don't want to have to rely on the factory preset.

MIX: You have a reputation for going into a studio and not coming out for days. How did you get into that habit?

POTOKER: That gets back to all the technology that's available. I like to explore all the options. Something might sound great, but I still want to know what it's going to sound like if I try another approach. I end up exhausting all the technical possibilities or exhausting myself, whichever comes first.

MIX: How do you approach a song?

POTOKER: It depends. Mixing is different from producing a song. When I'm producing a song from scratch, I'm afforded the luxury of reworking the parts. With album mixing, I'm a bit more confined by what's there on tape. In remixing, I'll pick out parts that I would really like to accent, develop or delete, maybe creating a sixteenth note on the hi-hat when it had an eighth-note feel, or doubling things up with harmonizing. I'll go in there and get a different perspective on the song. Usually people come to me because they've heard something I've done, they know what I'm capable of doing and they want something different. So I'm more or less given free rein. I'll just do what feels right.

▾▾▾

"There's so much to be said for live feel. Manufactured music isn't going to fool anybody."

PHIL RAMONE
A Legend
Continues to Grow

"*I've always thought that a producer's job is to be the objective director of action.*"

▼▼▼

BY DAN LEVITIN

PHIL RAMONE IS widely considered to be one of the great producers in rock. He has enjoyed long-lasting relationships with Paul Simon and Billy Joel and has worked with artists as notable and diverse as Paul McCartney, Bob Dylan, Lou Reed, Gloria Estefan and Barbra Streisand. In his 20-plus year career, he has received eight Grammies and 12 Grammy nominations (not counting those for artists he has produced), and records bearing the Ramone touch have sold (in aggregate) over 200 million copies worldwide.

▼▼▼

MIX: You recorded two albums for Dylan: *Blood on The Tracks* and *Before The Flood*. My perception of Dylan is that he seems to rely a great deal on inspiration and spontaneity in his performances. How do you create a well-crafted record with someone who's so spontaneous?

RAMONE: Dylan comes to the studio with what I call "prepared spontaneity." You never know what key he's going to play in or when he's going to play what. He performs in such a way that the first thing he does is what comes out most eloquently. He's not a guy you go in and overdub, so you just build the album around knowing that.

The first time I recorded him, he came in with a bass player and played the seven or eight songs he was going to do, front to back, with about an hour and a half of tape rolling. Then we talked to John Hammond and Don DeVito [CBS A&R men], and he went back out and did it again. Maybe the second time around the bass player played better notes. We chose what we liked. When he worked with Robbie Robertson and The Band, those things were choreographed, and yet a lot of it was left open, so that if he decided he wanted to sing another verse, he could do it.

MIX: Working with Paul Simon or Billy Joel has got to be very different…

RAMONE: Definitely. For one thing, with someone like Dylan you don't sit there with him during the writing process. He doesn't share that time with you, whereas they'll share unfinished songs—a missing verse, alternate chord ideas, things like that—with you. So you're a lot closer to what the songs are about.

MIX: Does that make you feel more removed from him?

RAMONE: No. Bob's a very nice man. He's not what you'd call a high-intensity conversationalist, but you don't need that. You have your moments of privacy with somebody and you enjoy them. But my way of working is not to break that code of professionalism and privacy that the artist sets up, whatever that may be. Dylan treats the people he works with in a completely professional manner. Sometimes the doctor-patient type thing is vital, so that you keep from getting too close. He shares what he needs to.

MIX: You've been with Billy Joel for over ten years and at least that many albums. In a case like that, does it become difficult maintaining distance?

RAMONE: You do grow closer personally. Billy's my child's godfather. And Paul Simon and I are still close friends—I named a son after him. But there is a line when you are employed by someone. You keep yourself somewhat at a distance so that they have it clear in their minds that you didn't party the last two nights because you had work to do, maybe some editing at eight the next morning that was more important. That's what I consider the proper relationship between an artist and a producer.

I've always thought that a producer's job is to be the objective director of action; you need to know what's going on with an artist because their emotional state may be reflected in their work, in the change of a lyric, for instance. But you get enough intimacy working with them ten and twelve hours a day in the studio. It's not always necessary to spend the weekend with them.

MIX: It must be kind of strange to get dumped when, after working with someone for a while, they move on to somebody else.

RAMONE: When the producer or artist makes a change, the work they did together remains.

MIX: There are three situations in particular I'm thinking of. *The Bridge* was one of Billy Joel's best albums, I thought, representing a new maturity in him as a songwriter. The three albums you did with Paul Simon, *Rhymin' Simon, Still Crazy* and *One Trick Pony,* were very important albums in his career. And many people think that *Blood on the Tracks* was the last great Dylan album. But each of these artists used someone else for their next record. Why do you think this happened, following such peaks in their careers?

RAMONE: Other than the obvious reason of a scheduling conflict, if artists take a new step forward, they are exploring a different reaction from the public as well as within themselves.

In Paul's case, after the soundtrack and the movie [*One Trick Pony*] came out, there were other things in the way of us working together, but we came back together to talk and work on certain things for *Graceland.*

You mentioned artistic maturity. The public's perception of that isn't always immediate. I thought *The Nylon Curtain* was one of the best things Billy had done, but a lot of people started calling it the Nylon *Shmata* [Yiddish for rag], which I thought was a terrible thing to say to someone who's bared his soul, writing for a year. If we had instead put out *Innocent Man II* or *Return of the Innocent Man,* I think *that* would have been a big failure.

The tragedy of it is, the record business demands that you have hits almost every time out. And if a producer has a relationship with someone over a number of years, at some point the time will come when someone, be it the artist or the producer, will say, "I think I'd better go make a move somewhere else."

Nothing lasts forever. Every time somebody calls me up and says, "I'd like to make another album with you," I'm like, "Oh! Well, great!"

MIX: What kind of training did you have as an engineer?

RAMONE: I was very lucky. There was a wonderful guy who taught me, Bill Schwartau. He was what I call a "seat of the pants" guy. And also, I was always tinkering. Sometimes I'd work all night and it would be five in the morning and what are you going to do then, go to a restaurant? The hell with that. I'd go in the room and start playing with bias on the tape. Because I was always fighting to find different ways to get better sounds.

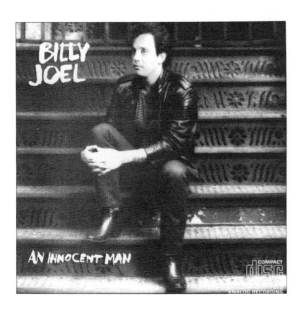

RAMONE HAS PRODUCED MANY OF BILLY JOEL'S ALBUMS, INCLUDING 1983'S "AN INNOCENT MAN"

MIX: Do you have some kind of bias trick that no one else knows about?

RAMONE: No, but I used to underbias my records to achieve a silkier top, but that means that you cannot plant +3s and +8s over zero onto that tape. One of the battles in the early days was with the old machines, the heat factor would mess everything up, so that what you mixed at eleven in the morning and came back to hear at six at night wouldn't be coming back off the tape machine the same. Now I'm a big Dolby SR fan. What I often do is record the drums at 15 ips SR, and then bump it over to digital. Digital solves so many of the problems I battled with trying to store information on tape. You put it there and it still sounds the same later on in the day or in the project.

MIX: How much attention do you pay to the sound of the console?

RAMONE: I use less console than anybody I know. I go right into the back of the machines; I'm a big fan of the Jensen preamps.

MIX: I read in George Martin's book [*Making Music*] that you were a child prodigy violinist. What made you give up the performing side of music?

RAMONE: When I was 12 or 13 years old, I believed that if you were going to perform, you had to be a superstar by the time you were 15 or 16. Playing jazz fiddle and rock 'n' roll fiddle—which I was trying to do—put such a limitation on me. So I went to work in a recording studio when I was 15, and by the time I was 18 I understood a lot more about electronics, and got much more fascinated by the sonic end of music.

MIX: You recorded some of Paul McCartney's *Ram* LP. When it came out, I thought it sounded the most like a Beatles record from an individual Beatle.

RAMONE: Yes. I was a big fan of McCartney's, of course, and of that first album of his, *McCartney,* that he did at his house on a Studer 4-track. When he was ready to do his next one, he called me up and we did it in New York.

MIX: One thing I'm curious about is the bass—Paul has this distinctive bass sound that carried over to *Ram* from the Beatles records.

RAMONE: Yeah, I remember that bass! We called down to the front desk at the studio and had them round up all the Pultecs they could get their hands on and every EQ in the place; we also got this UREI parametric equalizer. We just rolled up the bass on everything we could, as much as we could get on disc and know that the bass would be heard on radio.

MIX: Are there any artists/songwriters you like who you haven't already worked with?

RAMONE: Sineád O'Connor, Michael Penn, Vernon Reid, Michael Hutchence, Difford & Tilbrook, Melissa Etheridge. Rodney Crowell's work is wonderful. Another guy I think is brilliant is Lyle Lovett. I was a big fan of Lyle's; we were about to make a record and then the country people got scared that I would take him somewhere else.

MIX: But your career has been so diverse. Did they believe you can only do rock 'n' roll? In a period of only a few years, you worked with Kenny Loggins, David Sanborn, Dylan, Chicago, Quincy Jones, McCartney, The Band—all over the map. I can't imagine what the record company was thinking. You're…you're PHIL RAMONE. There was a punk band named after you…

RAMONE: I guess it depends on what kind of executive is in charge now. And Lyle's record would have been the perfect venture for me, you know, the "little big band"—that's the kind of thing I love to do.

MIX: What is your relationship with engineers when you're producing? How much do you get your hands in?

RAMONE: When I hire somebody, I want them to feel they can be creative and not intimidated. I'm only afraid when they say the same stuff I've heard for 15 years—"I must have my APIs, and I must have my little MXRs and I must have my tube mics." And I say, "Why? Why can't you survive with something that was built in 1988? Why are you relishing an old tube 47, which you're putting through this awful gain structure that just negates it?"

I'd sometimes rather pick an engineer who's been doing live, because they've had the experience of doing it every day, of miking real drums. And some of these guys that do monitor mixes are better mixers than the guy who's been doing the record! They've got their hands flying all over the place.

I look for young people. I like people with ballsy ideas. I like people who *understand* reverbs. My argument about reverb with most people is they spend all this money and they have all these racks and racks of stereo re-verbs, and everything is bouncing off of left and right. There's no discrete left, no discrete center and no discrete right a lot of the time, and that's when I get on their case. The whole point of all of this should be to create some emotional-sounding spaces. You can't do that unless you know how to use them. People should take the time to learn something about natural acoustics. The best use of the new toys is to really take advantage of spatial effects.

We used to have just EMT plates and rooms for 'verb. When that was all you had, you really needed to know how they worked. Digital has of course changed everything: Reverbs are cheap now. You can have a couple of 224s, a 480, some SPXs; it's a nightmare when I think back to how we made records before. It was archaic. But you know, some of those old records still sound good, and a lot of that was the engineers' familiarity with acoustics, with *real* sounds.

▼▼▼

> "**P**eople should take the time to learn something about natural acoustics. The best use of the new toys is to really take advantage of spatial effects."

RICK RUBIN
Forever Def

"I hate technically
slick records that have
no sense of emotion."

PRODUCER RICK RUBIN seems to revel in his controversial image. Staring menacingly out of his publicity shots like some demonic biker on acid, the 28-year-old co-founder of Def Jam and current owner of Def American Records is a self-made millionaire and self-taught studio pro whose current roster of acts (including Slayer, Andrew Dice Clay and Danzig) all seem guaranteed to upset the establishment. So it's a bit of a shock to find that in person, the man responsible for unleashing the Beastie Boys and the Geto Boys on an unsuspecting world is a soft-spoken pussycat whose Hollywood Hills home is full of Beatles CDs and books on the Fab Four. In this interview, he talks about his influences and his studio methods.

▼▼▼

MIX: What were your musical influences growing up?
RUBIN: Aerosmith was the first group I actively pursued. I was in junior high school, heard an album and then bought all of them. Before that, when I was real young, I listened to the Beatles a lot, although I didn't understand what I was listening to. But then, looking back, I'm really glad that I did, and I'm still a huge Beatles fan. After Aerosmith, I got into Ted Nugent and AC/DC, and then into punk rock—everything from Black Flag and the Circle Jerks to Discharge and Minor Threat. I also started listening to new wave music, such as Talking Heads, The Cars, The Ramones and Husker DÜ. At the same time, I'd gotten into funk, especially James Brown, so all of these influences kind of spread into each other. And then I started listening to rap a great deal when I was at high school, and by the time I got to college, I was listening exclusively to rap.
MIX: How did you get into the music business?
RUBIN: My parents' plan was that after college I'd go to law school, but instead I got into making records. At first it was strictly a hobby—I never intended it to become a business—but then we started selling a lot of records. My label at the time was called Def Jam, and I produced seven 12-inch singles that we released independently. In fact, I was running the company out of my dorm room at NYU, which wasn't so unusual. What was unusual is that the hobby grew into something so big, and then I was offered a production deal through CBS to form my own label. I'll never forget getting my first check from CBS, which was for just over $600,000, and I sent a photocopy to my parents and they said, "Okay, you have one year to be successful in the record business, and if not you have to go to law school." Luckily, it was a good year.
MIX: Your first single was "It's Yours" by T. La Rock and Jazzy Jay.

▼▼▼
BY IAIN BLAIR

How did you produce it without any training?

RUBIN: I'd recorded a couple of punk rock records before that, and I had a band called Hose when I was in college, and I put out a 12-inch and a 7-inch single, so I kind of had a feel for it. Also, I was deejaying at clubs, and I made friends with Ed Bauman at 999 Records who sort of walked me through the whole process, including how to get records pressed and where to go for mastering, etc. But in terms of production I knew very little.

As far as rap went, I thought all the records sounded musically just like disco, but then when I went to the clubs, I saw that rap was really a whole different sound. In clubs, with DJs scratching and mixing tracks—which was really a precursor to sampling—DJs were part of the record and sonic effect. They were the stars of rap, and as a fan I wanted to make records that reflected that sound. I think that when disco came along, it replaced funk as the black music label executives understood. So when rap came along, they used the same producers and the same old techniques to make rap records, but they were really still making disco records only with people rapping on them, which isn't what rap was about. So, being a fan and understanding what rap was really about, I tried to capture that on record, and ironically part of the answer was not knowing anything about the technology and what was considered "right" or "wrong" in the studio. It was about capturing some really awkward sounds at times. Looking back, they're pretty funny-sounding records, but that was what was going on.

MIX: How did you get involved with Run-D.M.C.?

RUBIN: My partner at Def Jam, Russell Simmons, is Run's brother, and when we had success with LL Cool J, he asked me to produce them. I was already friends with the band, and I'd played some guitar on their previous album.

MIX: How did you put together the famous Run-D.M.C./ Aerosmith collaboration on "Walk This Way"?

RUBIN: I'd finished the Run-D.M.C. *Raising Hell* album, which didn't have that track on it, and after listening to it thor-

Rick Rubin

oughly I called Russell and said, "It's good, but we need that little extra something to make it great." So I started looking for a great track to cover, and the moment I heard "Walk This Way" I knew that was it. It had a groove rap audiences would understand, and lyrically it was a song rap artists could deliver without much change. It really was a rap song. Looking back, I'm pleased because I feel it opened the eyes of both sides—rock and rap—and showed them that they're not so radically different after all. It's so strange to me when people say, "How can you produce rap and heavy metal? They're such opposites," because I don't see it that way at all. I think they're very much in tune with each other.

MIX: The Beastie Boys' *Licensed to Ill*, which you produced, broke a lot of new ground. Were you aware at the time what its impact would be?

RUBIN: No. We were just trying to make a great record, and it took a long time to make—nearly two years to complete. We'd cut a song or two every month. It was very casual, and I think that's why it has so much variety—the writing took so long.

MIX: What was the wildest thing you did on that record?

RUBIN: It was done long before the sampling craze started, and I'll never forget when we started recording at Chung King, my studio in Chinatown. We had tape loops going all over the studio. I got the guitarist from Slayer to do some solos, and he thought it was bizarre to be doing a rap record. Everyone thought I was nuts.

MIX: Even the Beastie Boys?

RUBIN: They hated it. There was a big fight, but luckily I prevailed.

MIX: How has living in L.A. affected your musical vision?

RUBIN: L.A.'s a very rock 'n' roll city versus New York, which isn't at all. New York's very Euro-disco: go to a club there and you hear house music and European dance music. In L.A., you hear Led Zeppelin, and you can go to clubs and see ten different bands in a night. I think it's great that that community exists, and I feel there's a very positive artistic community here, which I didn't feel in New York. The weird thing is I used to hate L.A., even though I came here all the time. Now I love it.

MIX: You admit to being a self-taught producer. Does that give you a different perspective on the job?

RUBIN: Definitely. I look at producing in a very different way from most other producers. I think of it as being more like the director of a film or a play. By that, I mean that for the technical side of it, I hire engineers who I think are competent, much like a director hiring a cinematographer, and I let them do their gig. That doesn't mean I don't have very strong ideas about what I want to hear, but I don't technically know all the bells and whistles to make it sound that way. I think the most important thing a producer can do is spend time getting the songs into shape before recording. The material is so much more important than the sounds.

MIX: Give us an example of that approach to a record.

RUBIN: I produced Red Hot Chili Peppers' *Blood Sugar Sex Magik*, and we were in pre-production for seven months, working on the material. Then we recorded the whole album in three or four weeks. The process of getting music onto tape is simple, but getting the music to the point where it's ready to be recorded is tough.

MIX: A lot of bands like to write in the studio.

RUBIN: I know, but I'm totally against that. The studio is not a place for writing. It's a place to make magic happen, not to think. I'm a huge fan of pre-production, and that should be done at home or in a rehearsal studio. So with this Chili Peppers album, we got the material to the point where, if I'd left the project before we recorded, and they'd basically kept to what we'd worked out over those seven months, I think the resulting album would have been the one I wanted.

MIX: What producers have influenced you?

RUBIN: I love the way the Beatles' records sound, and Led Zeppelin's, and I think Mutt Lange has made some amazing records: *Highway to Hell* [by AC/DC] is my all-time favorite. I like those old records best. Of the newer stuff, I like Lenny Kravitz's sound, although that's trying to sound like the '60s again. I like Jeff Lynne, too, though I'm not exactly sure why because I'm opposed to a lot of the stuff that happens on his albums. They're lighter-sounding and more processed than I'd like them to be, but he gets the best vocal sound. It's magical.

MIX: What engineers do you like to use?

RUBIN: My current engineer is Brendan O'Brien, who's younger and newer than my usual guys. I like to work with Jim Scott, Andy Wallice, Steve Ett, Dave Bianco. They get the sounds I want, although sometimes I have to argue to get them, because my ideas tend to go right against what's technically right. I just don't like the technology to dictate to me.

MIX: What studios do you like?

RUBIN: I don't really like studios, period. That's why I liked doing the Chili Peppers album in a house. If I have to go, I like Ocean Way and Hollywood Sound, which is a small, old, dumpy place with a great Neve board.

MIX: Since forming Def American and signing acts like the Geto Boys, Danzig and Slayer, you seem to have gone very hardcore.

RUBIN: I don't think I've changed that much. *Licensed to Ill* was a very aggressive record, as were LL Cool J's records. I've always made consistently aggressive records, both lyrically and sonically. At the same time, the label has the Black Crowes, so there's diversity there. The main thing for me is not to get stuck in a rut. That's why I stopped producing rap records. It just got tired and old. And that's why I had such problems with Geffen. They were very unhappy with me when I stopped making rap records. They didn't understand it at all. I've never made any records to capitalize on a trend, but labels don't think like that.

MIX: You've produced a wide variety of artists. Is there a "Rick Rubin sound"?

RUBIN: I think so, although it's easier for me to say what I don't like than what I do. I don't like reverb, and on the Chili Peppers record we didn't use any. That's very unusual, because most bands prefer to be enveloped in some reverb. I like to make dry records that capture a performance. I hate technically slick records that have no sense of emotion or of the artist's performance, and all of my records sound like the artists—whether it be the Beastie Boys or LL Cool J or The Cult or Slayer or the Masters of Reality. I'm not one of those producers who has a stock sound and then adds different personalities on the top as icing. I think I'm good at making very personal records for the artists.

▼▼▼

"*The studio is not a place for writing. It's a place to make magic happen, not to think. I'm a huge fan of pre-production, and that should be done at home or in a rehearsal studio.*"

SHEL TALMY
The '60s Hitmaker
Is Back

▼▼▼

BY BLAIR JACKSON

THE FIRST SURPRISE is that he isn't British. Despite making a name for himself producing a string of UK hits in the mid-'60s for such artists as The Kinks ("You Really Got Me," "All Day and All Night," "Tired of Waiting," etc.), The Who ("I Can't Explain," "My Generation," "The Kids Are Alright," etc.), the Manfred Mann Group ("The Mighty Quinn") and The Easybeats ("Friday on My Mind"), Shel Talmy is a Yank from Chicago. He also produced hits for Chad & Jeremy, albums for the great British folk group Pentangle, he "discovered" the 17-year-old British singer/songwriter Davy Jones (who went on to become David Bowie), and he was at the helm of albums by a number of other great but less heralded English artists like Bert Jansch, Roy Harper and Nicky Hopkins.

By the end of the '60s, though, Talmy had grown weary of the day-to-day grind of recording, and his work trailed off through the '70s as he became consumed by a number of other interests. He worked as music supervisor on several films (including *Butch Cassidy*), he dabbled in real estate, started a book publishing venture, wrote three adventure novels and also began a successful computer company involved with optical scanning and storage.

Still, he always kept up with changes in recording technology, and then, several years ago, he began recording bands again. A stint with The Fuzztones for RCA inaugurated the latest phase of his long, distinguished career. More recently, he was at the helm for a new album by the popular Milwaukee acoustic band Ecoteur (on Chameleon Records).

I talked to Talmy about some of his career highlights and about his decision to get back into music after an eight-year absence.

▼▼▼

MIX: Why did you decide to come back to producing, working with The Fuzztones?

TALMY: It's a simple and mundane answer: They approached me shortly after they'd signed to Beggar's Banquet Records. I listened to their tape, and I liked what they were doing a lot, so I thought it might be fun. And it was. I liked the label, too. They've been good at promoting their releases. Also, this came at a time when I had sold my interest [in the computer

company], and I frankly missed being around artistic people. That's something you just don't find as much in straight business. I ended up liking the experience so much I decided to go back into it full time.

MIX: I guess working with a raw band like that hasn't exactly thrust you into the world of digital recording.

TALMY: Hardly! They're really adherents to the '60s way of doing things. We were using Farfisas and old Vox amps that buzz like crazy, ancient guitars. It was great fun.

I want to be selective about who I work with. There's only so many records I can do a year, and I don't want to get into that thing of overcommitting by booking too many projects. So I've been moving slowly, letting the industry know I'm back producing again and seeing what develops.

MIX: Is it a liability that you haven't been around much, and that your name is so closely associated with artists from a specific time period so long ago?

TALMY: Oh, definitely. This is the sort of business where if you're out of it for a *year* people wonder if you're retired, and I hadn't done anything [in music] for about eight years. Personally, I'm trying not to look at this as a "comeback," because it's not like I was ever dismissed in the first place. I just got out of it. I got bored, I got burned out, and I thought I wouldn't return; but things change. The climate in the business has changed. I hear more bands playing straight-ahead, good songs, which is what I've always liked. Down here [L.A.], most of the bands I've seen are playing live without synthesizers, and they want to go into the studio and record live.

There's a move back to actual drummers, instead of machines. Those are all encouraging developments to me.

MIX: You made your name in England. Where did you get your training—Chicago?

TALMY: No, I only lived there until I was about 15. I got into recording after I moved to Southern California, where I worked in TV for a while, and eventually I met an engineer named Phil Yeend who had a studio called Conway, and he trained me. It was 3-track, and I picked up on it immediately. Three or four days later I was an engineer. I had always liked technical things, and I just took to it. This was 1960 or '61.

It was a good little studio. Phil was fairly avant-garde for that time. We did a lot of experimenting on separation of instruments, which hadn't been done much at that point. He would let me do whatever I wanted after our regular sessions were over, so I used to work out miking techniques for how to make drums sound better, or guitars sound better. A year or two earlier it was almost all mono, and engineers weren't that concerned about separation. So all the work we did there on separation held me in very good stead as the number of tracks available increased through the years. We weren't the only ones doing that, by any means. There were many good engineers around L.A. who recognized when 3-track came in that it was probably just the tip of the iceberg, and that both tape and recorders would continue to get more sophisticated. This is really even pre-transistors.

MIX: When you moved to Britain in the early '60s, what was happening musically over there?

TALMY: Very little. A lot of people were doing covers of American records, and there was a lot of local stuff that would obviously never make it out of the British Isles.

MIX: How did recording there differ at that time?

TALMY: It didn't differ much. The equipment was similar; everyone was using Ampex recorders and Altecs. I think EMI had some old Philips machines.

MIX: Most of the top producers in England worked with specific record companies, didn't they?

TALMY: That's right, and that meant that most of them were on salaries and not really getting royalties. I declared myself an independent producer when I arrived and got royalties from my first record, so I was always a little bit out of the system. I don't know if people resented me for that, or what. But I always got along well with other producers.

MIX: Were there specific producers who influenced your style?

TALMY: It's hard to say. I can honestly say I never heard a record and then said, "I want to use that drum sound on my next record." On the other hand, I was influenced by some records, like a Marty Robbins record that had the first fuzz guitar I'd ever heard. It happened by accident, apparently; there was a short in the amp, and the guitar made this distorted sound. Well, that was a real revelation to me.

But with the kind of music we were recording, there really weren't many precedents, so we were all doing it for the first time together. It was all totally new.

MIX: What was it about The Kinks that knocked you out originally?

TALMY: The songs—which is virtually where it started with everyone I've ever worked with. They were called "The Ravens" and had already been together a couple of years, and they were already quite good when I heard their acetate. They had this upper-class manager and were playing mainly debutante dances. [Laughs]

MIX: Did they pose any special challenge in the studio?

TALMY: Well, I don't know if Dave [Davies, lead guitarist] had heard the Marty Robbins record, but he sure loved fuzz guitar, and he used to slash the cones of his amp and kick it to get it as grungy-sounding as he could; and it certainly worked. They had great energy and a different sound than anyone I'd heard in England or the States at that point.

MIX: I have this sense of The Kinks, the Stones and the Beatles coursing together through the late '60s on similar but still different paths. Were you constantly checking out "the competition," seeing what new tricks George Martin came up with?

TALMY: Not really. I certainly admired his production; obviously, he knew how to make great records, but I didn't analyze it too much. As for the Stones, well, I thought the sound on their early records sucked, but they had something that was clearly unique. It was obvious they were a great band.

We all were aware of each other, and, of course, we all knew each other. At the beginning we were all a little naive, I think.

MIX: You didn't do much overdubbing, did you?

TALMY: As we got more tracks, we did more overdubbing, and I always liked to overdub voices. One of the things I started doing as an engineer was double-tracking voices. You talk about deficiencies in equipment and acoustics—these days you can go in, find all the dead spots and correct them in no time at all. But that wasn't the case in that era. It was trial and error, and so I discovered that double-tracking the voices let me fill in some of the holes in the sound. I'd also move the singers around the mic to alter the way it sounded in relation to the first track, to fill in the sound. I did that with The Bachelors, with The Kinks, virtually everyone.

MIX: Did you have to deal with many old-guard engineers during the early '60s?

TALMY: Oh sure, especially at Pye [Recording], where I did most of The Kinks' records. There were a couple of older guys there who really resented both the music and all of us, because we were all young. It was all crap as far as they were concerned, and they wanted to do big bands and ballads. However, a lot of younger engineers came on the scene right around that time. I still did a lot of my own engineering with The Kinks,

SHEL TALMY PRODUCED MANY CUTS
ON THE WHO'S "MEATY BEATY BIG
AND BOUNCY," INCLUDING "THE KIDS
ARE ALRIGHT" AND "MY GENERATION"

even though I was mainly producing, in part so I could have more control over my sessions. I'd hire a good assistant to do some things.

MIX: How involved was Ray Davies with the early Kinks records?

TALMY: Quite a lot. He was without a doubt the most prolific writer I've ever known. He'd come in with 30 songs that he'd written over a few days, and we'd go over the material—putting stuff aside for later, choosing what we'd do immediately. And then we'd talk extensively about the arrangements. I was always happy to hear what his ideas were because they were usually good.

MIX: Looking through your discography, it seems like you did an awful lot in a very short time. Was it actually a situation where you'd work with The Kinks one week, The Who the next and so on?

TALMY: At one point, yeah. It sounds more difficult than it actually was at the time. We were all young and full of energy and right in the middle of…well, I know you've read about the "swinging '60s" in London, but if you didn't actually experience them, it's hard to explain what they were like. They were *energy-filled*. Nobody got a lot of sleep, but nobody gave a damn. We all worked long into the night, and then we'd go out to parties.

MIX: So you socialized with the bands outside of the studio?

TALMY: No, I didn't really. We went to *different* parties. [Laughs] I always felt it was important for me to keep some distance from the people I worked with, though I must admit I now regret that decision. I wish I had spent more time socializing with them and getting to know them outside of work. I thought at the time it might not be good for the work, but now I believe the opposite.

MIX: You were with The Who during a brief but seminal period in their career. What ended your association with them?

TALMY: The Who were managed by a fellow named Kit Lambert, who was extremely jealous of anybody he thought was usurping his influence over the band. As a producer, of course, I *did* have some influence over them. From the first record, I made hits with them, but then one morning I got a letter from Kit saying, "Your services are no longer required." I didn't like that, and my contract didn't agree with that, so I sued him and won. Unfortunately, winning didn't mean that I got to record the group any more, and I've always been sorry about that.

To be fair, I think the group felt like they had to listen to Kit, because obviously he was great at PR and did a great job of marketing them. So if he said I was a bad guy, I guess they had to go along with that. I don't think they gave a lot of thought to it. They were very young; we all were.

MIX: What's the deal with Manfred Mann? I've liked a few songs, hated others, and I could never quite figure out who he was and what he brought to those records he did.

TALMY: That's a very good question. [Laughs] He's what people would now call "a concept man." The Manfred Mann Group was his band, to be sure, but his main strength was choosing other people's material and then knowing what to do with it to make it commercially palatable. Obviously, Dylan was a favorite of his, and he did very well with a few of his songs.

He brought a bunch of disparate personalities together so they could work together, though there were times when I felt like my role in the studio with them was as resident shrink. He was a strange guy in a lot of ways, but he was also very nice and bright, as were all the people in the band.

MIX: As an independent, did you have to be particularly budget-conscious?

TALMY: Absolutely. Either I worked for a company and was in charge of the budget, or I did it out of my own production company budget, like with The Who, where I put up the money myself. So I was very aware of what I was spending. With The Kinks, which Pye was initially funding, they had a real scumbag president who said that if we went one penny over budget, it would come from me, so I was under a lot of pressure.

MIX: Did you ever have any of those classic, late-'60s projects that went seven months longer than they were supposed to, and you wanted to put a calliope on this track but decided on a full string quartet instead?

TALMY: [Laughs] I saw it happening around me, but it never happened to me, thank God. I never had the patience for that kind of stuff.

Then and now, I've always tried to have everything pretty well worked out in advance in terms of the material and the arrangements. We'd work in rehearsal rooms and have it to about 90 percent of what we wanted when we actually recorded it. I don't like big surprises in the studio. I like to leave enough room for startling creativity if it happens, but it's still nice to know what you're doing. The studio is a place I like to *work*. It's not a place I like to eat and hang out and play pinball.

MIX: In the late '60s, you moved in more of a folk direction with Pentangle and Bert Jansch. Was that strange for you?

TALMY: No, it was great. I grew up loving folk music, so when I got the chance to work with some of the best people of the time, I jumped at it, and I loved doing it. They were all great musicians and real individualists, to say the least. It was a pleasure, and *Basket of Light* remains one of my favorite albums I've worked on.

MIX: You're returning to music in such a conservative climate in terms of what gets played on the radio. That must be a little frustrating for you.

TALMY: There isn't much good radio out there, it's true. Even here [in L.A.] it's hard to find a station that's at all adventurous. Fortunately, college radio seems to be filling the gap somewhat.

MIX: College radio may play The Fuzztones, but who's going to play the next Pentangle that comes along? There are entire genres of music now that can't find a home on radio.

TALMY: That's a good point. It *has* gotten narrower. But at the same time, things do break through, whether it's Tracy Chapman, who has helped get more folk music on the radio, or other people who are somewhat out of the mainstream. The fact is, you never know at any given time what's going to be popular.

MIX: So what's the answer as a producer? Be true to yourself and keep your fingers crossed?

TALMY: That sounds like pretty good advice. I've always tried to do work I could be proud of, and I expect to continue that way.

▼▼▼

"I don't like big surprises in the studio. I like to leave enough room for startling creativity if it happens, but it's still nice to know what you're doing."

CREED TAYLOR
Pride, Craftsmanship and All That Jazz

"I've never subscribed to that 'one microphone and let's get a natural mix' stuff."

▼▼▼

BY ROBIN TOLLESON

H E RANKS WITH the greatest of the jazz era. As much or more than Blue Note's Alfred Lion, Milestone's Orrin Keepnews, ECM's Manfred Eicher or Columbia's Teo Macero, Creed Taylor is the producer whose ideas about forming a band, shaping a sound and arranging a record date have influenced countless musicians and music lovers.

Think of the watershed tracks he was responsible for: Ray Charles' *Genius & Soul Equals Jazz* (Grammy winner); Stan Getz's "Desafinado"; the Getz-Gilberto "Girl from Ipanema" (another Producer of the Year award); Bill Evans' *Conversations With Myself*; Deodato's theme from *2001*, "Also Sprach Zarathustra"; Grover Washington Jr.'s *Mister Magic*; Esther Phillips' Grammy-winning, disco-pop groundbreaker "What a Difference a Day Makes"; and Freddie Hubbard's jazz gold, *Red Clay*. In an interview with Leonard Feather, Hubbard spoke of working with Taylor: "He's able to see how a real fusion can be made without sacrificing the music. He knows where people's heads are at, what tunes will click."

Taylor's hand helped shape memorable albums by John Coltrane (*Africa Brass*), Lambert, Hendricks & Ross (*Sing a Song of Basie*) and Quincy Jones with Mingus. "The first one Quincy did was called *This Is How I Feel About Jazz*," recalls Taylor, who's been involved in recording for several decades, but has lost none of his enthusiasm for music. "That one had Zoot, Milt Jackson, Mingus, a whole truckload of fantastic players. Every Wes Montgomery session was an event, and the Brazilian stuff was all exciting."

Looking at even a sketchy discography, the variety of music is startling—the subtle brilliance of Jim Hall's *Concierto*, with the rich tonal flavors of Paul Desmond and Chet Baker. There's Milt Jackson's graceful *Goodbye*, which captured the young flute talent Hubert Laws. Following Wes Montgomery, George Benson came on the scene, and a Best Producer and Best R&B Single Grammy for "Theme from Good King Bad." There were the days during the recording of *Out of the Cool* when he could

watch Gil Evans create arrangements on the spot with a whisper to a trumpet player or a note scratched hastily on a matchbook. There were albums by new artists like guitarist Allan Holdsworth (*Velvet Darkness*) and keyboardist Bob James in the mid-'70s, and a whole Brazilian pipeline of musicians during those days, thanks to arranger/keyboardist Eumir Deodato and percussionist Airto Moreira.

CTI, Taylor's label, has formed and honed some fine rhythm sections: Billy Cobham and Ron Carter, Grady Tate and Ray Brown, Steve Gadd and Will Lee. The arranging talents of Don Sebesky, Eumir Deodato and Bob James were brought to the public ear through the label; indeed, arrangements were custom-tailored for each artist. George Benson not only sang for the first time on the CTI label, but began working with live string sections, a practice he enjoys to this day.

The last record CTI put out before a five-year break in 1981 was an all-star session called *Fuse One*, featuring Stanley Clarke, Ronnie Foster, John McLaughlin and an emerging Wynton Marsalis. CTI ended the hiatus with a bang when it released *Rhythmstick*, which features another divine assemblage including Dizzy Gillespie, Tito Puente, Phil Woods, Art Farmer, "Smitty" Smith, Bernard Purdie and Charlie Haden.

▼▼▼

MIX: How did you get involved in the record business?

TAYLOR: I was a jazz lover from way back. I used to buy Blue Note and Prestige Records in 1945, when I was in high school in Virginia, and I listened to live broadcasts from Birdland. I went all over the place trying to find jazz records. You couldn't find them down South. But there was Symphony Sid every night from Birdland on the radio, so I heard all these great players, like Bird and Lester Young. I came up whenever I got the chance to go to Birdland and 52nd Street and that whole scene. And I played in high school and college. I went to Duke and played trumpet, and had a pretty good jazz band there. I got out of college and came to New York with plans to play. I ran into somebody who had just started a record company, and they weren't doing so well. They let me produce a couple albums, and they were both hits. One was Kai Winding and J.J. Johnson, the other was Chris Connor. That started the whole thing.

MIX: Had you spent time in the studio learning the tricks before you got your first producing gig?

TAYLOR: Really, I was just lucky. I fell into it, and I have pretty good ears. Having listened to records with such concentration, I knew what I could do that wasn't being done, hadn't been done, even though that Blue Note stuff was quite good. Rudy Van Gelder was the engineer even on those albums I was buying in high school. I would call them "non-productions." And I saw ways to make that kind of music more appealing. So it was really a seat-of-the-pants situation.

MIX: And by "non-production," you mean they'd just have the band show up and throw up a mic.

TAYLOR: Exactly. If they had a good day, you'd get a good record. If they had a bad day, they'd put it out anyway. Prestige would do that. Not so much Blue Note. I think they had a little more integrity. But generally speaking, most of the jazz of that era was non-produced, and not well-recorded, either.

MIX: Was that the state of the industry at that time, or was it more that way in jazz recordings?

TAYLOR: Well, jazz was such a stepchild art form at that point that the players were pretty much relegated to second-rate studios, and they weren't paid. Of course, when Norman Granz came along with Jazz at the Philharmonic, he gave good players a lot of work. And they were better off economically, but I don't believe artistically, because he didn't believe in *producing* records per se either. His philosophy was to give them as much freedom as possible. That has never been my approach, and the players who record with me or for me know at the outset that I'm an *active* producer. If there's a disagreement over a song or something like that, or somebody wants a D minor seventh in a certain place, I don't argue with that. But I like a relatively controlled audio environment. Certain bass players play well with certain drummers, and the same with keyboard players or horn players, and I like to mix and match and be actively involved.

MIX: Would you have suggestions regarding the personnel on the record?

TAYLOR: Oh sure, the personnel and/or arranger. And my sessions always have rehearsals *before* the studio, and then studio rehearsal also. And if we have a bad day, that bad day never sees the light of day. [Laughs] It remains on the cutting room floor, unless somebody comes along years later and happens to buy the company that owned the masters in the first place. That's a different situation.

MIX: Did you call artists who you personally liked?

TAYLOR: Yeah. I would say that's the case about 100 percent of the time, whether it's Wes Montgomery, George Benson, Quincy Jones, Ray Charles or Basie. I liked their music before I approached any of them about recording. And some of them I grew up with in the studio, like Quincy. He came to New York about the same time I did.

MIX: Did you find any musicians who rebelled against your way of working? Some might want more freedom in the studio.

TAYLOR: Generally, I wouldn't get involved with someone who felt any kind of reticence about going that route—the more controlled environment. Ornette Coleman and I would not get along very well, because he has a definite approach to music and recording that I'm not comfortable with. And actually Charlie Mingus would fall into the same category. Maybe Archie Shepp. I guess they were called "avant-garde."

MIX: I loved some of the young talent who developed out of the company. One of the first times I heard Steve Gadd play drums was on a CTI Milt Jackson record. And then the first time I heard Patti Austin was on your label.

TAYLOR: She had made some single records, but had never completed an album before. That was her first.

MIX: Did you enjoy working with the young talent?

TAYLOR: Absolutely. The thing about staying in the studio on a regular basis is that these new guys keep coming in to fill a chair. You hear them once and say, "Oh, that guy sounds pretty good." And then you think, "Maybe I should call him for this other type of date and see how he does on that." That's sort of the way it went with Grover Washington. He was a sideman for many CTI dates. When I got familiar with his playing and he was comfortable in the CTI environment, he started recording as a leader. The same thing with Bob James.

As far as the Brazilian artists were concerned, we had a conduit. Deodato had a big hit, and he started out strictly as an arranger for some of the Brazilian artists, like Astrud Gilberto. And he brought me Milton Nascimento. It was either Eumir Deodato who would bring in a Milton Nascimento, or Airto who would bring in different guitar players or keyboard players. So it really started happening that the musicians who were recording for CTI or whoever I was working with would say, "Why don't you come do this date? I think you might find it interesting to record with Creed."

It was a constant flow of new talent coming in via the studio recordings. And then for several years we promoted our own CTI All-Star concerts. That gave everybody under contract an opportunity to play live with other CTI artists. There was a camaraderie among all the players, not only in the studio, but also live.

MIX: Did you depend on your engineer a lot?

TAYLOR: Yes. The bulk of the recordings were with Rudy Van Gelder. It's almost like I don't have to say anything to him, and he doesn't have to say anything to me. We just nod. Over the years of working with somebody like that, you think like each other.

MIX: And you always knew going in that Rudy would be able to get the basic sounds you wanted.

TAYLOR: Yes. Over the years, he's constantly updated his outboard

> "If technology does something, the more the better. The only problem is that when the computer or the synthesizer starts taking over the tail is wagging the dog."

equipment. He stays pretty much on top of whatever's happening with the new technology. And there was another engineer I worked with a lot over the years: Phil Ramone. He did a Jobim album and the Astrud Gilberto-Stan Getz "Girl from Ipanema," and other good stuff at the Midtown Studios before they tore the building down. I did most of my work either there or at Rudy Van Gelder's, in Englewood Cliffs, N.J.

MIX: Your records not only sounded better than most of the other jazz releases in the '70s—you could hear each instrument—but they were also more accessible to the general public. Were those both goals of yours?

TAYLOR: Sure. Going in, I was making records I would like. And if I liked them, it followed that other people would like them. I avoided making records that radio would like to program. Early on, I did make some of those mistakes, because there was a certain predictable programming format you could follow to get on the air.

MIX: You worked with George Benson before he was a superstar.

TAYLOR: When I first started recording George, he was playing in the shadow of Wes [Montgomery]. Wes had just passed away, and George could play stuff like that. He didn't use his thumb like Wes did, but he could play octaves just as fast. But he wouldn't play them because Wes did that. After about a year, George loosened up and started playing anything he felt like playing. But in the beginning, he was so afraid that he would be doing what the master did.

MIX: He wasn't singing much at the time, was he?

TAYLOR: No, the first time he really sang was at a CTI concert at Carnegie Hall. He sang "Summertime," and I think that was the first time he did the vocal thing with the scat in the middle, and the audience loved it. But I never did feel like recording George as a vocalist. He was such a phenomenal guitar player. Now, oddly enough, he's having a problem. He was so big as a singer that he lost a real core of guitar fans. Now he's trying to get back into that idiom.

MIX: What do you think of the jazz records today, sound-wise?

TAYLOR: Technically, they're better. But are we talking on acoustic bass or synthesized bass? Or combination drum machine and live drummer? It really comes down to whether the music's good. If the music's good, it's sounding better today than ever before. I've never subscribed to that "one microphone and let's get a natural mix" stuff. If technology does something, the more the better. The only problem is that when the computer or the synthesizer starts taking over the tail is wagging the dog.

MIX: Are you a digital fan?

TAYLOR: Die-hard digital. And I'd better be, because otherwise I wouldn't get along with Rudy at all. He has absolutely slammed the door on analog. And he's a staunch supporter of DAT. He's absolutely right, because the technology is there. I mean, it sounds better than anything. The only time that digital is a problem, when a consumer might say an LP sounded better than a CD, is when the record company didn't make a transfer correctly. I would never take a 2-track analog mix of the stuff I have at Rudy's on 24-track analog and transfer it to digital. We would go back to the original 24-track and mix it through a PCM down to a new digital mix. Because, obviously, you've got a different set of problems. If it's digital, you have no worries about compression, tracking, nothing. You just open the thing up and make it sound good and that's the way it's going to be.

MIX: The other way sounds like cheating.

TAYLOR: It is. It's an expedient, economical way to send it through the system and wind up with a nice-looking CD. The transfer on *Blues and the Abstract Truth* should have been mixed down from the original 16-track analog to 2-track digital and then mastered. The same thing happened with the Jim Hall *Concierto* record transfer. CBS took the original 2-track analog and transferred it, and the 24-track was available. That's one of those uncontrollable, terrible things that happens in this business.

MIX: I'd like to talk about the CD entitled *Rhythmstick*. That was sort of the band name, too.

TAYLOR: Actually, the name comes from this stick that Dizzy has carried with him for years. It's made of old bottle caps, a broomstick sort of thing. And the players on the date, without having talked with each other, all came up with the same thematic premise: Dizzy Gillespie is the master of rhythm. People associate him with the bebop and the Charlie Parker thing, but actually he can solve any rhythmic problem under the sun. I hadn't realized what a natural rhythm analyst Dizzy is. Tito Puente and Smitty were having trouble on a new Afro-pop tune called "Wamba," and Airto was trying to help solve the thing. The time signature is 6/4, but it sounds like 3/4. Tito had something going that sounded like 9/8. We filmed all of this, and it shows Dizzy standing in front of the drum booth explaining to Smitty that if you do this little thing on the hi-hat and then kick the bass drum to get it right into the next bar…It sounded so simple the way he was explaining it, and once he explained, we got a take.

MIX: I understand you've started back up on the trumpet.

TAYLOR: I'm really enjoying it. I did some recording in the past, but who knows what lies in the future. It's feeling very good.

▼▼▼

WAS (NOT WAS)
Behavior Self

WAS (NOT WAS) is a new type of R&B—Rhythm & Balls. As your feet take control and run off dancing, your brain gets whiplash from the lyrics. It's as smooth as buttered buns; it's zany on the edge. Their eclectic and critically acclaimed *What Up, Dog?* album featured the Top 10 dance hit "Walk the Dinosaur," the caressive "Spy in the House of Love" and "Wedding Vows in Vegas," crooned by Frank Sinatra Jr. With Don and David Was masterminding, and soul stunners Sir Harry Bowens and Sweet Pea Atkinson interpreting most of the material, Was (Not Was) has at times enlisted the vocal chords of Mitch Ryder, Ozzy Osbourne and Mel Torme.

Beyond their unique blend of well-lubricated soul and neo-beatnik outbursts, what surprising and godfatherly producing we get! Bonnie Raitt's *Nick of Time* is an album that sounds good the first time you hear it and winks from the turntable, "You wanna hear it again?" And over here we've got Don cranking the propeller on the B-52's, and off they go with a "Love Shack" roar. Back there Don and David watch over the historic Roy Orbison/k.d.lang "Crying" session. Then comes Iggy Pop via Don, and Bob Dylan with both Was' at the producing helm. Most recently, Bonnie Raitt's *Luck of the Draw* zoomed up the charts with Don behind the helm.

▼▼▼

BONZAI: What is the first music you remember—the first song that got to you?

DON WAS: There is a great irony here. The first music I remember hearing was the Broadway cast album of *The Pajama Game*, which my mother played incessantly. It was John Raitt singing, "Hey there, you with the stars in your eyes" that got me. When I first met Bonnie she had me call her dad's answering machine, and he sang that line and then said, "Hi, we're not home now…" I got my mother to call long distance so she could hear it.

BONZAI: The song had a profound effect on you?

DON WAS: Well, maybe I felt the need to come back later in life and pay the debt. It probably had no effect on me at all, but it's the first song I remember hearing.

BONZAI: Who was your first teacher?

DON WAS: I'm pretty unschooled, actually. My dad went out to the Jewish community center once in 1955 and came back with this old guitar he bought for three dollars. He tried taking lessons, but he could not grasp it. Out of curiosity, I asked him what he didn't understand. He showed me a D chord and a G chord and the guitar was mine after that.

BONZAI: Who showed you that music could be fun?

▼▼▼

BY MR. BONZAI

DON WAS: I had a terrible music education, but there was one piano teacher who I really liked. His name was Murray Jackman, and he played the piano bar at the Playboy Club. He was a great influence on me.

I only took three lessons with him, because I didn't like the discipline of learning scales. I only wanted to play what I felt like playing, and he was the one who said, "Okay, just do it." He explained that everything had chords, and if you are going to play a C chord, you might as well be playing *West Side Story* as Mozart. He gave me that greater picture. I took music classes at the University of Michigan, but I didn't get it. It seemed like everyone was preoccupied with moving up in the hierarchy of the music department. I never cracked the code.

DAVID (LEFT) AND DON WAS

BONZAI: You were a music major?

DON WAS: Yes, but just for a minute and then I split. I knew exactly what I wanted to do and it wasn't happening there.

BONZAI: What exactly did you want to do?

DON WAS: Precisely what I am doing now. Precisely. It's pretty amazing. I've done this record with Bob Dylan, and that's exactly what I wanted to do: produce Bob Dylan records. Pretty incredible, and it's been a long time, too. That was 20 years ago.

BONZAI: You've picked some gentlemen to interpret your music in such a soul-searching way—Sir Harry Bowens and Sweet Pea Atkinson. Is it true that they first thought your material was "sick"?

DON WAS: Yes, that's one of the words they've used. But there was a good bond among the four of us from the very beginning. I don't know that they were completely tuned into our nuances, and we certainly weren't totally tuned into theirs. I don't think they got a lot of the stuff, which is the charm of the records. Sweet Pea is not really trying to interpret those lyrics; he runs them through the soul computer.

BONZAI: The words are so great, and they come out so well with their voices. Rhymes like "big producer, cheap seducer."

DON WAS: Those are all David's lines. He's an incredible writer. He really hits that borderline. Another step and it would be comical, like Tom Lehrer. He never ventures beyond; he never loses the poetry of it, and yet he pushes it to the extreme. He approaches from such a cockeyed stance and view of life. And I don't just mean songwriting.

BONZAI: I must admit I have laughed while listening to the song "Zaz Turned Blue." It's out there.

DON WAS: The desired reaction was that people would start laughing, but the smile would slowly slide off your face. You'd think maybe he's serious. "What is this?" That's the ultimate reaction. If people can ask that question, then I think we've made some successful music. The people I admire are the ones who have defied categorization. The stuff that lasts is clearly that.

BONZAI: *What Up, Dog?* was named one of *Rolling Stone*'s Top 100 albums

DON WAS (LEFT) AND ENGINEER ED
CHERNEY SHARE A QUIET MOMENT IN
THE STUDIO

of the decade, but it probably doesn't fit most record companies' concepts of a consistent sound.

DON WAS: Yes, we've been called "marketing nightmares" to our faces. If you really stop to worry about that you'll make some boring records, and you may sell some.

People who are inspirational to me are guys like Leonard Cohen and people outside of music—filmmakers, novelists. It doesn't matter if they are trendy or not. They do a body of work. Some things are better done than others, but if you are looking for a 25-year run at the stuff, you better lift yourself out of this trend thing or you go down with it.

BONZAI: Another cut, "Can't Turn You Loose." I love it when Sweet Pea has to quiet the band down. And the audience is going nuts, like at a James Brown concert. Was that really recorded live?

DON WAS: No, not in concert. If the truth be told, the applause comes from a Tears For Fears record. You should have been with us the day we recorded. We were on a frantic search in London for some applause. We searched through the tape vaults, and finally our A&R man, who also works with Tears for Fears, said, "Wait a minute, I can get some applause for you." He bailed us out.

It felt live; it was recorded live in one take and everyone was playing at once. We just needed something to cover up a little tape hiss and thought, "Why not?"

BONZAI: Tell me about the 12-inch remix you did for the Rolling Stones' "Rock and a Hard Place." Why you?

DON WAS: I don't know why me. Mick Jagger is a very cool guy, by the way. I read all the stories and expected a prima donna to be on the other end of the line, but he was courteous and intelligent. He was in the middle of doing this tour, with shows that were as elaborate as anything that has ever been performed. And he still had time to do a lot of work on this 12-inch. He phoned in, took updates every two hours.

"Rock and a Hard Place" is 140 beats per minute. He said he wanted it to be played in dance clubs. I said, "Nothing at 140 beats gets played." So we did an elaborate procedure on it, slowing it down to 120 beats a minute. Of course, everything was unlistenable. We had to find the proper harmonizer to bring the voices and guitars up to pitch. Once we did that, we called a drummer named Pat Mastalatto. He came in and beat a quarter note to the track on the bass drum, because the time moves around—it's where the feeling of the thing comes from. Once we had quarter notes laid down, we hooked up the Human Clock and replaced all the drums and bass and added keyboards. There's even a mix with no guitars. We did a straight club thing. A pretty outrageous overhaul.

Frankly, as a Rolling Stones fan, if I had heard it I would have hated it. But I did what I thought was necessary to have it played in a club. That was my portfolio. At the end, Mick Jagger called up and said, "You did everything I asked you to do, and I really hate this." I said I understood and suggested he go test it in a club. His calls started trickling in, leaving messages, mentioning things he sort of liked. He was really sweet and was trying hard to like this thing. "That section there with the repeat voices, that's good."

They pressed records, but I think it's too radical a departure. I don't think they shipped many records, and no one has ever said anything to me about it. I don't think people have heard it. It's a pretty interesting record.

BONZAI: Did *Nick of Time* have a big effect on your career?

DON WAS: The biggest effect has been learning the value of live rhythm dates. I never did live rhythm dates before — I'm an overdub baby. I crossed an important threshold when I learned that you don't listen to a rhythm date the same way you do to overdubs that you're putting into a sequencer. You gotta see the forest and not examine each tree. It's difficult to do, but somewhere in the middle of that album, it made sense to me.

From that point on, I've really enjoyed doing rhythm dates. It underscored the most basic thing. If you find a good song and sing it well, people will respond to it. You can get lost in the digital delays and all the other stuff. For me, the importance in that album was learning restraint. People talk about Sonny Rollins and how the spaces are as important as the notes. It's the same in producing that record — the holes in there. It gave me a little courage to keep it bare.

BONZAI: Do you have a distinct idea in mind when you start a producing project, or does it come in the ensuing chemistry?

DON WAS: I'm loathe to go into something if I can't hear it first. It's like Hitchcock, who used to do elaborate planning. I don't go to that extent, where I have to hear every guitar part beforehand, but if I can't imagine what the overall texture will be, I figure I have nothing to offer. That is the luxury of having success with Bonnie's record. I can now actually go after people who I have a feeling for. I worked with Iggy Pop, and I grew up on The Stooges. They played at my high school. I knew what his records should sound like before I met him. I was hoping I'd get a chance to produce him, and I met him a year ago. It seemed very natural, and the record is what I hoped for.

I think you go in as a fan. That's the best producer — someone who is a fan. If you are a teenager and you're waiting for the next Duran Duran or Beatles record, you're hoping it's going to be a certain way. You can hear it in your head. I used to dream the next Bob Dylan album, the next Beatles album. I wish I could have woken up and written down the songs. I dreamed whole Beatles songs that never existed, because I was so excited about what was coming next. A producer should have the same enthusiasm — the same insight.

BONZAI: Did Dylan come to you, or did you come to Dylan?

DON WAS: I guess he came to me. I met him last summer. Afterward, I got a matter-of-fact phone call from someone in his organization: "Bob was wondering if you would work on a song." It was pretty cool. We did one song with Stevie Ray Vaughn, Jimmy Vaughn, David Lindley and Kenny Aronoff. It worked out well, and we went ahead with the album. Listen, let's get back to the studio — you gotta talk with David.

[I later had the opportunity to speak with David and Don together.]

BONZAI: This "Was (Not Was)" name has not been explained to me.

DAVID WAS: It's the distributive principle, actually. As in "Was (Not Was) = Was Not + Was²." It's sort of algebraic.

DON WAS: We took our monikers in the same sense as if the Beatles had called themselves "John Beatle," "Paul Beatle."

BONZAI: And there is some flexibility there, too. I noticed on one album

"I don't think computers are musical. What they do is remember 10,000 DX7 settings better than humans."
— Don Was

you are known as Don St. Was and David St. Was.

DAVID WAS: We went to Geffen Records and we thought that with the label's classy image, we should class our act up, so we took on the aristocratic "St." names.

BONZAI: What can computers do better than humans, musically?

DON WAS: I don't think computers are musical. What they do is remember 10,000 DX7 settings better than humans.

DAVID WAS: Computers are so rigid in the music-making process; if you are after something that reflects the coldness and the alienation of being in a world that is dominated by things, then you can take advantage of them. I had my best luck with sequencers when I turned the volume down while I played and created a groove. It's like throwing Velcro notes against a Velcro catcher's glove. Without intelligence or reason, this thing snags onto little impulses you make with your hands. I've always insisted that if you put a family of gorillas in a room for six months with some good electronic gear, they would come up with Prince's *The Black Album*.

BONZAI: David, you were once a jazz critic.

DAVID WAS: Yes, on my way to somewhere else. I never really meant to be one, and I apologize to the world for being one.

DON WAS: I think you only need apologize to Chick Corea, who you so mercilessly lambasted.

DAVID WAS: Well, he wasn't alone. Chick, I apologize.

BONZAI: Was this to make money?

DAVID WAS: It was basically to not work and make money. I just continued the same lifestyle I had led throughout my adolescent years with this fine gentleman. Being a jazz critic is like going to art school. It was an art school without walls. Meeting these guys who we'd grown up revering and mythologizing—Miles and Ornette, Jelly Roll Morton. It was like—what did Dylan say about Woody Guthrie?

DON WAS: You mean about never brushing his teeth?

DAVID WAS: Yes, but he also spoke of the end of idolatry. By meeting them, it makes artists not only human, but less than human. You see that all the pieces don't have to be there. Genius isn't a function of mental or physical health, but of the missing piece in the puzzle of these personalities. That's what made them unique—their limitations.

BONZAI: Don, 20 years ago you knew what you wanted to be doing today. How about you, David?

DAVID WAS: I suppose not. I came from a family of actors and that seemed like a pretty good job to me. I grew up with the stage and figured I'd be doing that. Slowly but surely, I wiped it out of my banks because it seemed like a dumb profession. Not a heck of a lot of room for playing the theater in America. You wind up on *Alf*.

BONZAI: So music was your next goal?

DAVID WAS: Well, I met Don when he was playing the junior high talent show, doing a crude impression of Dylan. I had never heard of Dylan at 11 years old and took Don to be the real thing. Later on, naturally, I was bitterly disappointed. But I did fall under the sway of music and started studying and quitting every major instrument in the orchestra by the time I was 18.

BONZAI: Do these Was (Not Was) albums make any money?

[Both laugh]

DON WAS: No, not really, but the last one sold a few.

> *"Working on* Nick of Time *taught me that you don't listen to a live rhythm date the same way you do to overdubs you're putting into a sequencer. You gotta see the forest and not examine each tree."*
> —Don Was

BONZAI: How do you pay all the people who are on your records? I've never seen such humongous credit lists. Great artists, too.

DAVID WAS: We're like a benevolent association. Sort of a soup kitchen. We've kept a lot of people alive. It's the most satisfying thing about our work.

BONZAI: David, are you the main lyricist in the group?

DAVID WAS: Yes, but Don is my editor. He will edit a song from three pieces laying around in three different rooms. Bing, bing, bing—all of a sudden you've got "Yesterday," "Stardust."

BONZAI: Do people think you are brothers?

DON WAS: People think we are brothers, and they think we are black. They think we're Harry and Sweet Pea. Usually, when I meet people for the first time in person they think I am my own lawyer.

BONZAI: Do either of you sing on any of your records?

DON WAS: David does all the spoken word vocals.

BONZAI: What's this I hear about a new artist you are working with, Natalie Archangel?

DON WAS: She's very talented. She and her A&R man at MCA Records approached me about producing. They played some of her songs for me, and one of them was clearly an homage to the Four Seasons. It seemed as if you ran all of the Four Seasons songs into a computer and came up with the sum total, you'd come up with this track called "My Older Lover." So, I thought, why don't we get Frankie Valli to sing it with Natalie? Great video—Frankie playing the older lover. And he was very receptive to it.

BONZAI: Isn't this wonderful that you can just call people up and say, "I've got a great idea!"

DON WAS: It's the coolest, yeah. The very first record I ever bought was "Candy Girl." When you get a familiar voice in the studio and you're testing the mic before you run the track and you hear this voice that you know—it sends shivers up and down the spine. I experienced one such shiver with Frankie when he started singing. He sounds as good as ever.

BONZAI: What a way to start out the decade, huh? You guys are on the top of the heap!

DON WAS: Watch out—he's setting us up for something.

BONZAI: No, no. I was just wondering—do you ever wake up and fear that the ice is suddenly thin and the whole success will come crashing down?

DON WAS: I think everything is cyclical. You look at a kid like Boy George, for example. He experienced a bit of a collapse and took it to heart. I think if you examine anyone who is in this business for the long run, they have their ups and downs. I expect our success to last for another good week, and beyond that I'm not too worried. I think we know what we're doing now. If you know what you're doing and you have something to say, trends can't take that away from you.

DAVID WAS: There were so many times when we should have fallen through the ice and didn't. You don't expect to drown any more and are constantly surprised by things working out. You begin to trust yourself a little more. It's what you are doing that makes it happen, and not being the Tiffany of the week. We've been rolling for ten years like this, so I guess it could only get better.

▼▼▼

Photo Credits

cover photos *(clockwise)*: Jeffrey Katz; courtesy of Solid State Logic Inc.; Hideo Oida; courtesy of Solid State Logic Inc.

page v, Elizabeth Annas

page 2, used with permission of Sony Music Entertainment

page 8, Virginia Lee Hunter

page 12, Henry Diltz

page 15, Dennis Keeley

page 16, Dennis Keeley

page 19, Robert Kappa

page 21, Robert Kappa

page 22, Robert Kappa

page 31, Jeff Stacey

page 32, used with permission of Sony Music Entertainment

page 34, Peter Monroe

page 37, Sue Gold

page 38, Sue Gold

page 51, Thi-Linh Le

page 53, Thi-Linh Le

page 57, Blair Jackson

page 61, Andy Earle

page 62, Caroline Greyshock

page 64, Andy Earle

page 66, Ed Colver

page 69, Hideo Oida for both photographs

page 77, Rick Diamond

page 84, courtesy of Solid State Logic Inc.

page 87, Mr. Bonzai

page 89, Elizabeth Annas

page 90, Elizabeth Annas

page 93, courtesy of Solid State Logic Inc.

page 94, used with permission of Sony Music Entertainment

page 98, Peter Anderson

page 101, Roman Salicki

page 102, Roman Salicki

page 113, Mr. Bonzai

page 114, Elizabeth Annas